PRAISE FOR TRAVEL WISE

"*Travel Wise: How to Be Safe, Savvy and Secure Abroad* is a most valuable reference book for the experienced as well as the novice sojourner. As an international business professional who has traveled the world for the last 40 years I find author Ray Leki's book to be right on point. It is comprehensive, readable and informative, even for the experienced traveler. His personal and professional experiences come across in a clear and useful manner."

> —William R. Sheridan,
> Vice President-International
> Human Resource Services,
> National Foreign Trade Council

"Safe, savvy and secure traveling is essential in today's world. Ray Leki draws on his 20 years of international travel experience to show corporate and government employees, as well as the casual traveler, how to assess and mitigate threats and operate successfully in our new and sometimes dangerous cross-cultural world. With humor, insights and hundreds of real-life examples drawn from his own experience, Leki shows us how to cross borders and safely navigate the world. Essential reading for anyone who carries a passport."

> —Laurette Bennhold-Samaan, Sr.
> Manager Global Mobility, Accenture Ltd

"Combining traditional security awareness, cross-cultural, and interpersonal skills with proven emotional intelligence concepts; Ray Leki's *Travel Wise* Model offers an innovative and relevant primer for 21st century Globe Trotters! *Travel Wise* is a must-read for novice and seasoned travelers alike."

> —David J. Benson,
> Senior Diplomatic Security Special Agent (Retired),
> Former Director of the Diplomatic Security
> Training Center

"*Travel Wise* has a wealth of wisdom and information that will serve experts and novices alike. I use this material in my research, intercultural training programs and graduate courses. I recommend it to all, and thank Ray for doing a great service to the intercultural community."

—Professor Dharm P. S. Bhawuk,
Shidler College of Business,
University of Hawaiʻi, Manoa

"*Travel Wise* provides a holistic, frank and intelligent approach to safe travel and raises the bar for preparation and competency for personal safety and security. No matter your level of travel expertise, Ray Leki presents information to make smart, thoughtful and well-informed decisions."

—Nancy R. Lockwood, MA, SPHR, GPHR,
Senior HR professional, researcher and author

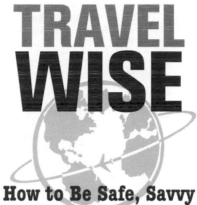

TRAVEL WISE

How to Be Safe, Savvy and Secure Abroad

Ray S. Leki

INTERCULTURAL PRESS
A Nicholas Brealey Publishing Company

BOSTON • LONDON

First published by Intercultural Press, a division of Nicholas Brealey Publishing, in 2008.

Intercultural Press,
a division of Nicholas Brealey Publishing
20 Park Plaza, Suite 1115A
Boston, MA 02116, USA
Tel: + 617-523-3801
Fax: + 617-523-3708
www.interculturalpress.com

Nicholas Brealey Publishing
3-5 Spafield Street, Clerkenwell
London, EC1R 4QB, UK
Tel: +44-(0)-207-239-0360
Fax: +44-(0)-207-239-0370
www.nicholasbrealey.com

The views and opinions expressed in this book do not necessarily reflect the views or opinions of the U.S. Department of State.

Printed in the United States of America

12   11   10   09   08   1 2   3   4   5

ISBN: 978-1-931930-36-9

Library of Congress Cataloging-in-Publication Data

Leki, Ray S.
   Travel wise : how to be safe, savvy and secure abroad / Ray S. Leki.
      p. cm.
   Includes bibliographical references.
   1. Travel.   I. Title.

G155.A1L432 2008
613.6'8—dc22

2008011947

*To all those who empower global peace and understanding through
venturing out beyond their homes to succeed in strange lands;
and to all those who fret over, protect, guide, inspire, and
lead them on the way toward international and
intercultural understanding.*

ACKNOWLEDGMENTS

This book wouldn't exist without the interest and creative vision of Intercultural Press Publisher Trish O'Hare. Her guidance, extraordinary skill, and patience in dealing with a fledgling author are what we all deserve though almost none of us gets. I thank her for her friendship, trust, encouragement, and dynamite feedback. All of the good people at Nicholas Brealey Publishing and Intercultural Press manifest her qualities and commitment to excellence and I thank them.

The original idea for this book came from a project that I started with my friend, former boss at the State Department's Overseas Briefing Center, and Peace Corps sister Lee Lacy. Our efforts to co-author this book in the early '90s as the reality of a global age spread like wildfire were sabotaged by overwhelming professional and family commitments in both of our lives. Our shared vision of helping people stay safe while getting the job done internationally lives on through this book.

Other friends and colleagues played invaluable roles in getting author, idea, pen, paper, and publisher together. They include long-time esteemed collaborators and professional colleagues Judee Blohm, intercultural beacon Gary Weaver of American University, friends and colleagues at the Foreign Service Institute, and many students and Peace Corps Volunteers who urged the book into being. My good friend DPS Bhawuk, who provided invaluable help in independently field testing the Travel Wise survey with his international business graduate students at the University of Hawaii shows me again what the wonderful Nepali concept of a *meet saThi* means. My amazing sister Ilona, who can teach rocks to write and proofreads with amazing insight, wit, and laser-like clarity, shares the credit along with my editors for turning my manuscript into something far more readable, with less frequent wild fluctuations in tense, voice, and grammar. I thank them. Ambassador Prudence "Pru" Bushnell is an extraordinary friend and American hero whose name and story I wish were part of every household in the land. She has taught us more about courage and empathetic leadership by her example than can ever possibly be gleaned from the mountains of books with the word "leadership" in their titles. Her Foreword is a gift that I cherish and hope whets the reader's appetite for the book she will one day write on her extraordinary voyage through her life.

In particular, I'd like to thank three amazing, brilliant, gorgeous women who provided invaluable advice through sharing their personal experiences and strategies for success while traveling the globe: Angela Witte, Theresa Caragol, and LeAnne Cummings. There are too many colleagues who shared ideas or encouragement over the past three decades for me to remember and acknowledge them all, but I must mention inimitable WWII flyboy and POW Claude Watkins, security pro Ed Lee, and my close friend and Cold War superspy Marino "Dorsey" Endrizzi, who with humor, wit, courage, and unflappable poise served his country with humility and an amazing moral compass.

Finally, I am surrounded by love and support on the home front: my high school girlfriend-turned life partner Cindy Blanchard Leki, and our daughters Janine and Jasmin, who gave me the time, space, and reason to focus on this book. They are destined to live truly global lives. Girls, if you wind up writing a sequel, promise me you won't call it: *Daughter of Travel Wise.*

CONTENTS

FOREWORD

"Code Orange" signs around airports and other facilities make me crazy. Indicating that we face a middling chance of a terrorist attack, an event the vast majority of humankind has not nor ever will encounter, these signs tell me nothing about what to do with this information. A weather report sends me to the hall closet, flashing lights on my car dash board, to a mechanic. But a threat level? I am stymied. Just as I am when people ask me, as a veteran Foreign Service officer and former ambassador, if I would recommend country X as a safe place to travel. I cannot tell you whether to travel to country X any more than I can predict that a Code Orange will or will not turn into a real event.

Life provides no guarantees, but that does not mean we need to go through it casting our lot to the fates or hoping the bad guys will stay away for another day. There are things we can do to travel wisely in the face of the unpredictable and if you prefer action over fearfulness, read on. *Travel Wise* asks the questions, tells the stories, and provides the information that will allow you to decide for yourself whether you (your loved one, friend, or employee) are prepared for the challenges and wonders of travel. In these pages, Ray Leki has gleaned lessons, wisdom, and street smarts acquired by the experiences of countless travelers and international organizations and reframed them for your benefit.

I grew up in Germany, France, Pakistan, and Iran. I understood that it was up to me to adapt to these worlds, not the other way around. I adjusted to the languages, picked up cultural cues, and watched others' reactions carefully so I would not make the same mistake twice. I considered these survival mechanisms; Ray presents them as skills and competencies. You do not have to trip over the rocks I and others found in our journeys to learn the same lessons.

The fact that many of these competencies can be learned is an important point that Ray makes repeatedly. I eventually made a career of the Foreign Service and, as a woman in a traditionally male profession serving in patriarchal cultures, had to discover tactics to overcome stereotypes and prejudice. I did not like it when I first met an important contact in India in the mid-1980's who greeted me with disdain and practically spat the words, "I can't believe the United States of America would send a *woman* to do this job," but I knew I had to learn how to help him deal with me. The fact is, as soon as you step out of your own culture, you are playing by someone else's rules, and the sooner you know what they are and how to play successfully, the better off you will be. Ray provides good insight into assessing cultural cues and using helpful strategies. (As for my rejoinder to the Indian man, I cheerfully pointed out that India had chosen a *woman,* Indira Gandhi, for the job of Prime Minister, so there should not be a problem.)

Attitude and expectation have a huge impact on the ease with which one learns competencies, and tolerates difficulties in the meantime. Ray's personal inventory questions and profile discussion will make you aware of the behavioral and psychological baggage you, like everyone else, carry with you. Countries to which my husband and I were assigned—Senegal, India, Kenya, and Guatemala—offered both hardships and opportunities. The aspects on which people chose to focus determined the quality of their experience. The large embassy in Nairobi, Kenya, for example, included Americans from a variety of fields and backgrounds. People who had served in other parts of Africa considered Kenya as close to heaven as they could come. Others, particularly those prepared for a first-world experience, found countless reasons to be unhappy. The place was the same; yet, expectations and attitude made it a great posting for some and a horrible one for others. As ambassador, the only thing I could do was to help create a community environment in which people could *choose* to be happy, or at least feel marginally satisfied. The rest was up to them. I found the same to be true in Guatemala, our next post.

The purpose of increasing awareness about your attitudes, expectations, and competencies is to maximize your ability to stay safe and secure, the ultimate goal of *Travel Wise*. So, let me get back to my frustration with Code Orange for a minute. For the first two years in my tenure as ambassador, Nairobi was deemed a "medium threat" post when it came to the possibility of a terrorist attack—not high enough to warrant a significant response to our security concerns about our building's vulnerabilities. Medium threat turned into dead-on reality on August 7, 1998 when al Qaeda dispatched truck bombs to the U.S. embassies in Kenya and Tanzania. Over 200 Kenyans, Tanzanians, and Americans were killed in those attacks and over 500 people were injured. A medium chance for the occurrence of any disaster, natural or manmade, demands thoughtful preparation. The discussions and case studies Ray presents come from actual accounts, with lessons learned the hard, even tragic, way. Whatever your experience as a world traveler, know that when you read Ray's examples and recommendations you are getting the insights of someone who has spent over 20 years developing and improving the security programs the Department of State provides to civilian family members headed overseas.

In the wake of the bombing in Nairobi, I saw people pick themselves up, re-establish their organizations, assist others as best they could, and help one another to heal far away from basic services we take for granted in the United States. Human beings are extraordinarily resilient, particularly when they approach difficulties as a community that shares trust. One can create trust and community anywhere, but it takes effort. It is worth making it.

Now, as a private citizen, I still love to travel. Oh, I know that bad things happen and that my vulnerability increases in foreign places. But I also know myself, how to take care and to avoid risky situations. Experience tells me that the odds are far greater that I will meet terrific people and enjoy wonderful adventures. I just need to be prepared—and so do you. *Travel Wise* is going to help. Bon Voyage.

—Prudence Bushnell, Former U.S. Ambassador to Kenya and Guatemala, March 2008

INTRODUCTION

A New Way to Look at Travel Safety

There is just no stopping us now—we've become a planet of globe trotters: we no longer cling to the land the way our predecessors did. If anything is already distinctly different about this young millennium, it is that we are truly each other's neighbors. Neither oceans, mountains, deserts, national boundaries, nor distances can keep us apart.

In many cultures it is now regarded as the norm to have teenagers spend a semester or year studying abroad, and international experience is widely regarded as a fundamental part of a well-rounded education. Almost every business organization of any size understands and appreciates that its long-term success lies in the global marketplace. Fluency in multiple languages is regarded more as an artifact of modern survival than an indicator of advanced intellectual curiosity and discipline. Government agencies at all levels recognize and cater to an international audience beyond their inherent parochial and traditional constituencies. Learning to move effectively through lands and cultures has become the new competence.

This book uses what I call the Travel Wise Model, a paradigm that will help you understand the full range of dynamics at play when you, your loved one, or your organizations struggle to evaluate the risk involved and perhaps prepare for an international adventure. The Travel Wise Personal Inventory in Chapter 2 helps you assess your readiness for travel based on a number of specific and idiosyncratic criteria. Then, with a solid understanding of where you stand against some of those criteria, the following chapters look at the components of the Travel Wise Model in more detail, letting you see where your strengths are and pinpoint needs for further attention. These chapters explore strategies for minimizing the risk and maximizing the gain in your travels, including tips to increase your travel competence and skill.

LEARNING TO SPEAK THE SAME LANGUAGE

Let's look at some definitions that will be helpful to keep in mind as you read this book. For example, what do you consider the difference between safety and security? Both words invoke a desirable state—a freedom from threat. But the words, at least as used in this book, are not synonymous.

- Safety: Freedom from threats that occur as a result of living in the world, including natural disasters, accidents, disease and sickness, natural death, and other sources of unintended but serious potential harm.
- Security: Freedom from hostile acts, including crime, war, harassment, intimidation, discrimination, and in the extreme case, genocide.
- Threat: Any occurrence, situation, or potential action that puts one's safety and/or security into jeopardy.
- Risk: An assessment of the probability and consequences/impact of a particular threat.

- Behavior: An individual's specific words and actions in response to stimuli encountered in day-to-day life.

With these definitions as a starting point, you can start exploring the dynamics of what happens to raise—or lower—the threat profile of an individual, group, or organization when leaving the predictability of home behind and embarking on a journey to a different cultural milieu. It might be useful for some to understand a bit about my background—to allow me to introduce myself and to help you connect a person with the ideas you will encounter in this book. (If that isn't a need of yours, please skip to the next section in this chapter.)

MY BACKGROUND

For more than 25 years, I've been involved in helping people maximize the success of their international travels—mostly with diplomats, development workers, students, government employees, and family members—but also with businesspeople and missionaries. I have worked with tens of thousands of sojourners to increase their chances for success in their missions—as students, workers, negotiators, soldiers, diplomats, plant managers, and tourists.

As a professor and government trainer and program manager, I help people evaluate information about the threats they might face, as well as the strengths and vulnerabilities they bring with themselves. Then I help them analyze the risks. But before I can help people analyze their risk, they need to really understand what the value of the trip is to them—the importance of their mission.

I began paying attention to personal and organizational security in a limited way as a Peace Corps volunteer. In September of 1979, I headed off with some 40 fellow volunteer trainees from John F. Kennedy Airport in New York City toward Kathmandu, Nepal. Along the way, the lumbering Pan Am Boeing 747 made stops in West Germany and touched down in Tehran while that country was seething and simmering in Islamic revolution. As the plane refueled on the tarmac, revolutionary guards toting M-16 assault rifles came aboard the plane and conducted some sort of "Welcome to Iran" search and intimidation activity. Two months later, a new era in international security would begin as students and security personnel in Iran took over the American embassy and held more than 50 diplomats—protected by international convention—hostage for the next 444 days.

As a 23-year-old Peace Corps volunteer, I was assigned by the government of Nepal to teach high school math and science in a remote village in the far northeastern corner of the country. While I lived in that little village in the mountains, seemingly on the other side of time, the Soviets sent their army into Afghanistan, at the western end of the Himalayas. At the northeastern edge of Asia, the "beloved" North Korean dictator Kim Il Sung's government sent glossy brochures to my students describing the wonders of economic and social development under his realm. Political instability in Nepal had the embassies of all of the various aid donor countries wondering how they could evacuate their development workers should the civil unrest turn violent.

There were no roads to where I was stationed. My closest compatriots included a British doctor in the district center, which was a day's walk from my village, and a free-spirited German water systems engineer who no one knew how to keep track of, much less evacuate. The nearest telephone and road were days away. My embassy sent me a helpful note suggesting that if the political situation in my village got rough, I should consider "walking due north into China (Tibet) and requesting political protection from the nearest border security personnel." As naive and inexperienced as I was, even I knew that would have been an unworkable idea. But it certainly made me consider my personal safety and security, the mission of my organization, and my assumptions about the ways the world worked from an entirely new and fundamentally different point of view.

North to China? Would there be a bigger threat to my security posed by local manifestations of civil unrest in my village than there would be from the obvious physical safety threat posed by crossing Himalayan passes at 17,000 feet (5,200 meters), and then stumbling along into some tired, cold, armed, scared (I happen to look a little like Yeti, the famed Abominable Snowman) Chinese border guards and explaining to them in my nonexistent Chinese that I could use a little help getting to Peking (Beijing)? This was one of those times that following instructions—something which I would generally recommend—just was not going to work. So what would I do?

Since I had no real way of understanding or predicting what civil unrest would look like in my village in this remote corner of Nepal, I decided to take stock of whatever I did know about. What did I have going for me? What capabilities and resources did I have?

I had considered myself a pretty good trekker, but I had painfully learned that any five-year-old boy or girl in my village could both outwalk me and more successfully navigate disappearing mountain jungle trails—particularly in the rain—when I had gotten lost during a three-day trek to another district center for a meeting. In a downpour of a monsoon rain that turned every drainage gully into what looked like a footpath, I found myself covered in leeches, and my legs and arms covered in welts from the stinging nettles that grew everywhere. Then a log bridge I was crossing collapsed and sent me hurtling down 10 feet on top of my backpack and sleeping bag into a stream.

Lost, bloody, leeched, welted, and now dragging a soaking backpack and sleeping bag, I began feeling pretty sorry for myself. It was getting dark, and the only direction I could tell for sure anymore was going downward. So I followed that stream until I came upon a small clearing where a young guy and his little sister were tending their family's grazing animals. I must have looked quite a sight—the little girl's face first took on a look of pure terror, and then as I came closer, she started laughing as she recognized me as a school teacher. That wasn't the highpoint of my trekking, clearly, but it taught me that going out into new territory in those mountain jungles wasn't my forte. So my only source of possible evacuation mobility—my legs and trekking skill—was a dubious potential strength.

I had, however, been fortunate in having formed some very good friendships with my neighbors and fellow teachers at the high school. Their sense of responsibility toward me was profound. This may sound silly, perhaps, but beyond being a novel amusement to the villagers, students, and teachers, they were proud that their village had a real, live (gigantic, hairy-armed, and blue-eyed!) American in their village. "Is it true Americans have been on the moon? Have you been on the moon?" I was a source of all sorts of entertainment. And the grateful beneficiary of remarkable decency and generosity. Villagers would give me whatever excess crop or fruit they had managed to eke out of that nearly vertical soil they lived on. Thinking I was lonely, the older men in the village would sometimes assemble in my little house just to keep me company and good-humoredly marvel at the amazing and unending difficulties I had keeping a fire going in the little *chulo*—the fire pit inside the house used for cooking.

I began to realize that the biggest resource I had, which the people in our embassy who sent me that evacuation suggestion had no way of knowing, was the loyalty and affection of this remarkable group of people living in this mountainside village. I had nothing to worry about from civil unrest inside or outside of Nepal: These people had an overwhelming hospitality and sense of compassion, gratitude, and responsibility, and they would protect me. With that resolved in my mind, I didn't pay one more whit of attention to political unrest and instead focused on being an effective teacher—that was my mission. This story underscores the basic idea of this book and points out many of the ideas I would use later as a traveler myself and as a manager of and consultant to development programs, internationally focused graduate students, diplomats, government employees, and family members.

WHERE TO START?

The question of motivation is fundamental to risk calculations, but also dictates the final terms against which success or failure will be measured. Inevitably, though, when considering our safety and security, we focus our preparations on what we know about wherever it is we are heading. That makes sense—only the foolish go to a place like Port Moresby, Papua New Guinea, without carefully researching the threats they are likely to face. But taking a step back and asking why we travel in the first place gives us a chance to better understand the trade-offs we will face in our journeys.

Financial reward may play some role in the calculation, but it is rarely the only source of motivation. Other reasons might include the prospect of an interesting or important professional challenge, the prospects for career enhancement, an opportunity to pursue an interest in travel and the languages and culture in the region, or a compelling stake in a personal friendship with someone who invites you. And, of course, some basic human needs may be involved: the need to feel useful; the need for companionship, love, and respect; the need to feel that one's life matters; and the knowledge that ripe opportunities for personal fulfillment involving international travel aren't always obvious or available in our day-to-day lives.

Although this might seem slightly counterintuitive, a clear-eyed assessment of the benefit is one of the first steps in analyzing the risk of an international project or mission. Most commonly, a combination of motivational factors are at play, and this complicates efforts to completely understand the potential value of the trip. Even if it is impossible to grasp what the potential benefits might be, just understanding the depth—or shallowness—of one's motivations is a big step forward in terms of analyzing the risk. (Chapter 8 focuses on making sense of the various motivational forces at play.)

WHAT'S IN THIS BOOK

So what can you learn that you can then apply to help inform the decisions that you will face—for yourself or those who you love and care about, or those organizations and personnel for whom you are responsible—as you embark on the journeys of an international life in this global age?

This book is about more than security and learning about cross-cultural competence, emotional intelligence, the right attitude, the right training, and the right approach. It is also about understanding who you are, what resources and limitations you bring with you, and how self-aware you are about your mission and what you are willing to risk to achieve your personal goals and those of your organization. In *Travel Wise*, you start by analyzing internal factors and then explore the external factors that confront you and perhaps your organization.

Chapter 1 introduces the Travel Wise Model and discusses how it empowers rational decision making and preparation towards a successful sojourn abroad. The questions in the Travel Wise Personal Inventory in Chapter 2 help you assess your readiness for travel based on a number of specific and idiosyncratic criteria. Chapters 3 through 8 help you put your answers to the questions in Chapter 2 in the context of the Travel Wise Model: your personal and interpersonal skills, cross-cultural skills, basic security competence, as well as understanding your motivations to travel.

Chapter 9 focuses on the organizational context. Whether you are in corporate security, international HR, or business planning for a corporation; are running a student exchange or study abroad program of some sort; or are in the international NGO arena and struggling to make sense of trying to protect people and a mission when your accountability and responsibility are very high but actual authority to control events on the ground might be very low, you will find a model to formulate your thinking and help guide your decision making. You get a chance to try out your new skills in Chapter 10 as you read about real-life situations as well as fictitious scenarios in the case studies. The Special Issues section following Chapter 10 considers some special cases, including student abroad programs, traveling with pets, and strategies for minimizing the often difficult task of coming home. The appendix will help you continue your Travel Wise learning and to develop a vast network of resources for country specific threat information so that, wherever your travels take you, you will know how to prepare yourself for success.

CHAPTER 1

The Travel Wise Model

You will never look at travel in the same way—yours or anyone else's. You will know the questions to ask, and the steps to take to prepare. You will understand how to increase—greatly increase—your odds for success in all of your adventures abroad.

The Travel Wise Model combines security awareness with cross-cultural skills, emotional intelligence, and other personal and interpersonal capabilities and balances risk and motivation so that both the external threat and asset environment—and the internal one—are exposed to create a new kind of intelligence specific to the individual, the organization, and the mission.

For the moment, consider the external threat. There are clearly some places on earth that present a great deal of real danger to any and all who live or travel there. Currently, for example, most of Iraq is such a place. Travelers headed to Iraq understand that there is considerable risk involved. Some go because of a sense of loyalty (the returning diaspora of Iraqi nationals who fled during Saddam Hussein's regime and want to rebuild their country, for example). Some go because it is their duty—soldiers who are given orders and are not in a position to choose whether they will or will not go. Some go because of the professional challenge and opportunity— journalists, diplomats, and aid workers, for example. Others are drawn by the lucrative financial benefits such a location offers: mercenaries, security personnel, and contractors all hoping to exact maximum financial gain without loss of their own freedom or safety. Others, believe it or not, are simply adventurers, and follow a compulsion few of the rest of us will ever fully understand to travel to such places.

WORKING THROUGH THE DECISION PROCESS

But how do we decide whether to go? What criteria do we use to analyze and weigh the benefits against the risks? Let's look at an example. An American professor is asked to go to Beirut to deliver a series of lectures and workshops. This would be a good professional opportunity, but she wonders whether it is safe to go to Lebanon—she remembers the pictures and stories of the Israeli invasion of southern Lebanon, and she understands that wars are inherently destabilizing for societies. But things seem to have settled down—Lebanon hasn't been in the headlines for months. So, is it safe?

A useful way to rephrase that question might be: *For whom might it be reasonably safe to travel to Lebanon at this time?* That's an entirely different question and one that can only be intelligently answered by understanding two sets of information. The first set deals with information about the traveler—her motivation, experience, capabilities, resources, and skills and competence as an international traveler. The second set of information deals with the reality on the ground in Lebanon today, and with the risk that is involved in getting there and back.

Lebanon—and specifically Beirut—is still a dangerous place to be. Active terrorist organizations that have headquarters there do not particularly like America or Americans. While the days of large numbers of American and European hostages (including academics) seem to have ended, at least symbolically, with the release of journalist Terry Anderson in December of 1991, the second Iraq War and the upswing in violence between Israel and Palestine have greatly heightened tensions recently. Moreover, Beirut is still rebuilding from the years of civil war that devastated the city. The recent Israeli incursion and the subsequent mass exodus of foreigners and Lebanese, as well as the ongoing tensions between Lebanon and Syria, are real sources of civil and political instability.

It is entirely predictable that in societies undergoing civil and political unrest, the basic infrastructure of a government's role in protecting people may be damaged, inchoate, or in a state of chaos. So not only are the external factors a potential source of threat, but the lack of a competent, reliable, and developed law enforcement and judicial system becomes a serious area of concern as well.

One way to understand risk is to imagine the worst thing that can happen and try to formulate a realistic approximation of the likelihood of it happening. Then try to imagine a much wider and broader set of more likely problems and threats that may be encountered and determine if any of those are "deal breakers." This process is essentially the same for individuals and for organizations, and will be detailed in Chapter 7 for individuals and in Chapter 9 for organizations.

Now, getting back to the academic who is considering the trip to Beirut: What's the worst thing that can happen to her in Beirut? She might be taken hostage and held for ransom or, if terrorism is involved, be held—or killed—for political gain. The probability of that happening is certainly small, but it does exist. A question for her to consider then is if she, as did Terry Anderson and so many others, had to languish in some form of horrid hostile detention (and almost all detention seems hostile and is horrid), would she feel that she had made a reasonable gamble and decision, or would she be plagued by self-recrimination, remorse, and doubt? In other words, if in her mind the value of the trip is worth the cost of her life—or at least her freedom—then it might be worth the risk to go. If not, it is difficult to understand why she should go.

But given this thought process, couldn't we then put every aspect of life up for evaluation against the direst of consequences and become immobilized by fear and fatalism? Is it worth my life to go to the corner coffee shop and risk getting run over, mugged, or poisoned to get a cup of coffee? Sure—particularly if the coffee is really good and the probability of any of those threats actually occurring is minimal. As is the case for the professor going to Beirut.

Additionally, though, travelers need to examine and evaluate the wider, more probable threats that might occur. Being robbed or mugged, for example, is a more likely risk. Getting off a flight at Beirut's Rafic Hariri International Airport puts any traveler at immediately greater risk. The surge of people in the arrival area and the inherent confusion of lots of tired people looking for luggage make these travelers good targets for criminals. Another invasion/ incursion or politically inspired car bomb blast might initiate another evacuation of Americans, Europeans, and other foreigners— an extremely disruptive, inconvenient, expensive, and probably uncomfortable scenario, but not life-threatening for the vast majority involved. And at the far end of the spectrum, a possible yet entirely benign and mundane risk might be that the lectures and workshops that originally prompted the trip turn out to be poorly attended or received, or just boring and unrewarding. How is that a danger? A boring lecture might not be a threat to one's security, but if the motivation that drove the professor to accept the invitation to go to Lebanon to do the lecture was centered around a professional challenge, the disappointment she might feel should become part of the risk analysis—it wasn't worth the risk even though nothing bad happened.

On the other hand, there are some people for whom almost every calculation will result in a decision that the potential gain is worth the risk, regardless of the desperateness or danger of the destination. Two of the terrible stories of loss amongst the countless in Iraq in the last few years serve as examples. The first was the death of senior U.N. diplomat Sergio Vieira de Mello, a Brazilian, who was killed in a bomb blast directed at the U.N. headquarters in Iraq in August of 2003. De Mello was a widely respected man of peace for whom the dangers were abundantly clear. He went because he felt his calling in life was to serve as an instrument of peace. Friends and colleagues throughout the international diplomatic community mourned the loss of this courageous human being and the senselessness of the killing, but few question his motivation or his decision.

Similarly, former Peace Corps volunteer, lawyer, and human rights activist Fern Holland lost her life in a hail of automatic weapons fire in an ambush in southern Iraq. She had dedicated her life to peace and women's rights, and well understood that as a Western woman in Iraq, even clad in an *abaya* and *burkha*, she would be in real danger and a glaring target. She was much beloved—like de Mello—attractive, charming, and intensely dedicated—and dead at 33.

KEEPING THINGS IN PERSPECTIVE

Deciding whether it is safe to go to the corner for coffee against the backdrop of the stories of de Mello and Holland helps restore a sense of perspective. Most of us are reasonably safe and secure in our daily responsibilities, routines, and travels. It is an easy and straightforward task to analyze the risk we face in our lives if we never go much farther than to the corner for coffee.

But today, for students, tourists, businesspeople, international development workers, diplomats, and military personnel, the assessment of risk can be a much trickier process. Add to that the reality that we are all blinded by our own desires—our hopes and aspirations obscure our ability to objectively evaluate risk. We tend to overestimate the value of a sojourn because we *want* to go. Similarly, we tend to underestimate the threats posed, even in the rare instances in which we take the time to understand those threats fully in the first place, because we unconsciously are trying to skew the data in favor of what we want to happen. A student eager to spend a semester on a kibbutz in Israel really isn't in a good position to make a rational choice. Similarly, the parents of that student may be frightened by the prospect of danger for their child and will tend to exaggerate the threats posed ("Suicide bombers are blowing up pizzerias and shopping malls every day!") while minimizing the value to the student (the possibility of an amazing cross-cultural and personal adventure and the opportunity to develop a sense of self-confidence, independence, and world citizenship in addition to personal development and growth).

So the conversations in that family over this highly desired (to the student) and highly threatening (for the parents) sojourn are not likely to be based on reasonable analysis unless both sides can step back and work together to gather information on threats, share feelings on their respective perceptions of the trip's value, and then come to some negotiated understanding of the risk. A Dutch firm contemplating an investment in Timor-Leste (East Timor) needs to go through the same process to evaluate the risk—and guard against overenthusiastic assessments of the prospect of profit against the potential for an expensive—and potentially embarrassing—failed venture.

DEVELOPING TRAVEL SKILLS AND COMPETENCIES

So far we've been talking about threats as local phenomena that have to do exclusively with the external security situation in the target country. The reality, of course, is that much of the relevant information on threats comes from a better understanding of the internal capacities—and liabilities—of the sojourner.

So what can you do to help inform the decisions that you will face—for yourself or those who you love and care about, or those organizations and personnel for whom you are responsible—as you embark on the journeys of an international life in a global age? You need to adapt and use a whole new range of skills and competencies in this truly global era. But what are these new competencies you need, how do you get them, and how do they fit together?

As most people now commonly acknowledge, cross-cultural skills are important. And given global jitters over terrorism and a steady increase in crime in urban areas around the planet, it would be equally difficult to find anyone denying the need for safety and security competence. Each of us can reach into our own well of personal experiences for examples of unfortunate lapses of another area of competence that common sense alone would dictate as necessary for success in an international environment—highly developed personal and interpersonal skills. It seems obvious that to be effective in an overseas adventure, as in almost anything else in life, everyone would be well served by being crystal clear on their motivation for going overseas in the first place. But international effectiveness goes beyond listing the desired attributes of travelers: these competencies are dynamic and interact in ways that are not obvious. Competent travelers and expatriates have an enormous synergistic edge in the global arena.

The problem of becoming a competent global traveler is one of awareness and balance. After watching a great number of people each year go overseas and return, some successful and some not so, certain trends become obvious to me. Some people are naturals—they can go anywhere, get along, take care of themselves, and get even the most complex jobs done. They are effective and they succeed. And there are others, at all levels of rank, stature, age, and international experience, who are train wrecks waiting to happen. Most of us plow through our international sorties somewhere in between.

Perhaps those travelers who seem to be "naturals" have a psychological predisposition to a complementary personality type, an awareness of their own emotional (particularly fear) states and other personal characteristics that incline them to be successful overseas. But to bring that latent skill into the realm of effectiveness, they—consciously or unconsciously—develop skills and competencies that facilitate their success.

Luckily, those skills and competencies are trainable and learnable. From missionary kids and semester-abroad students to ambassadors, business champions to tourists, and Peace Corps volunteers to overseas retirees, the same complex of competences either conspire for success or betray toward failure. While some develop these skills naturally, others can benefit greatly from wrestling with and gaining an understanding of the underlying dynamics, and using that understanding to shape their own attitudes, behaviors, and proclivity towards success.

INTRODUCING THE TRAVEL WISE MODEL

The Travel Wise Model integrates personal and interpersonal skills, cross-cultural competencies, security awareness, and motivation into an interactive matrix that helps travelers unearth information on risk, and thereby sheds light on how to mitigate the threats involved and maximize the potential for success. It helps travelers analyze, predict, and diagnose problems they may encounter while achieving missions abroad.

The value in the model is that it brings together the major components of threat to a successful mission overseas, whatever that mission may be, so that the sources of risk can be identified and managed. From this more comprehensive and holistic approach, it becomes possible to provide better preparation and support to ensure mission success.

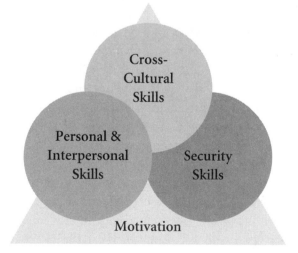

The model graphic demonstrates both the interactivity of the three skill domains: security, personal and interpersonal, and cross-cultural and the reality that those skills are built upon a bedrock of motivation. Without the motivation, the skills are academic. The skill domains are mutually enhancing—the greater the individual's personal and interpersonal skills, the greater the potential for cross-cultural awareness and effectiveness, which enables security competence. And a person who is secure and protected and not facing undue threat, nor the consequences of a safety or security incident is likely to be much more receptive to further learning, performance, and effectiveness in the personal/interpersonal and cross-cultural domains. And that cycle of effectiveness drills back down into the base of the model and greatly enhances mission success—the motivation for which the travel was undertaken.

What prevents us all from developing these skills? The same reality that is our biggest strength: the very person who holds that passport. Our fears, excitement, denial, and lack of awareness—and, in some cases, lack of doing our homework—collude to limit our effectiveness. Understanding and using the Travel Wise Model will help you to break beyond those limits.

COMBINING THE MODEL WITH SECURITY PERSPECTIVES

Serious interculturists around the world often lament the general public's lack of diligent interest in developing *culture-generic* cross-cultural skills and *culture-specific* awareness. To the intercultural researcher, the international day begins and ends in intercultural communication and a deep understanding of all that happens both above and below the cultural iceberg. To truly know another people and another culture requires understanding the central *raison d'etre* of the culture itself—why did the culture develop the way it did, with the assumptions, beliefs, and ways of processing life unique to that group of people? Language fluency becomes an invaluable window not just into countless cultural idioms and expressions, but into the ways a group of people think as well. But travelers often feel they don't have the time for all of that in-depth study and wonder about the value in dedicating time to understand abstract concepts like individualism, collectivism, locus of control, and other such arcane topics.

International security professionals are tortured souls caught in an eternal high-stakes poker game that they can never completely win and from which they can only, at best, contain any potential damage to their organizations. Through the lens of the security professional, the very risk that allows the opportunity for success carries with it dire and devastating consequences that need to be avoided and contained at all costs. But no one is interested in spending limitless amounts of money—not regional vice presidents, ambassadors, vacationers, students—to guarantee safety; they just want to focus on getting their respective "jobs" done. However, "getting the job done" means exposure to threat, and threats are what security pros spend their days trying to minimize. To a security pro, the exemplary overseas traveler or employee is someone who finds a way to get the job done while minimizing exposure to that great flux of threats that imperil the security of the mission. And they have a good point.

But what's the point of going overseas if the very contact we seek needs to be limited because of security considerations? How is the mission to succeed?

And how can personal and interpersonal skills help keep us safe and secure? A good example of how this comes into play comes from a discussion I had with an international human resource vice president for a large U.S.-based multinational corporation. We were talking about the need to screen and select people for international success. She said, "The reality is that there are people I am processing to go overseas who are being sent because no one gets along with the person in domestic operations. The corporation is trying to export the person in hopes that somehow he will succeed in Quanzhou. However, if he can't figure out how to get along with his peers and subordinates in Detroit, how the heck is he going to figure that out in Quanzhou? When this fails, of course, will management look at whose crazy decision it was to select this person to send to China? No, they will figure that somehow we didn't have the right cross-cultural training in place." If an employee has difficulties getting along and communicating in his own culture, how can he possibly succeed abroad when he will also not know the subtleties of another culture, society, and workforce?

If overseas success is linked entirely to the attributes of the traveler, why don't organizations just limit travel to those who have demonstrated their international savvy? Moreover, how can we know if the risk inherent in leaving one's own culture is worth it?

There is only one way to get one's analytical arms around this. The value of the voyage needs to be determined. That might sound crazy, but bear with me. Let's say a college language department is considering offering to take its highest-performing, highest-potential language students on a six-week excursion/ immersion tour of a country that represents the target language and culture that the students are studying. Unfortunately, the country is experiencing significant civil unrest and a general breakdown of law and order. What had been a paradise has become a dicey destination. How can university officials decide whether the benefits outweigh the risks? Even before the risks are thoroughly enumerated and researched, and plans and strategies are put forth to mitigate the risk, the sponsors of the trip must identify and articulate a clear, compelling value for the trip—in this case, a value that cannot be obtained by any other means. Perhaps the trip is designed to interest undergraduates in pursuing graduate studies in that field, or to reward or motivate them in their academic pursuits. Maybe the trip serves as an introduction to field research methods.

In the end, the value of the trip—this specific mission overseas—needs to be widely understood, desired, and accepted. Only then can the counterbalancing force—the risk—be weighed with any reason. One way to weigh and measure that risk is to ask, "What's the worst that can happen? And if it did happen, would our mission have been worth the risk?" (A tragic example of a miscalculation in risk and mission value analysis concerning St. Mary's College in Maryland will be reviewed in Chapter 10.)

So how can you be sure that this model—cross-cultural, security, personal and interpersonal competence, and motivation—is the right mix of factors for international success? There are different ways to verify this. First, let's look at the empirical response of international corporations and see what they have done to ensure their own international competence. Then we'll look at it through the eyes of a sojourner preparing for an exciting—and perhaps a little dangerous—adventure overseas. Both methods will lead us to the same set of conclusions and help understand the basic root idea of this book—that we need new skills—to be effective players in this wild and wonderful, new, truly international age.

Considering the Model from a Corporation's Viewpoint

Almost any international corporation of any size has a corporate security division. The security division is typically responsible for running a series of programs to protect the corporation from both safety and security challenges—running the gamut from developing hurricane preparedness to making sure intellectual property and trade secrets aren't stolen or resources embezzled.

Similarly, big organizations tend to have large human resource or human capital departments that might include an international division. These professionals have the task of preparing and managing international expatriations—sending an employee and his/her family overseas, including everything from providing assistance selling a home, arranging for language and cross-cultural training, packing and shipping belongings and furniture, locating a suitable living situation in the destination country, assisting and facilitating inpatriation, exploring employment options for a spouse, formulating and administering appropriate salary, compensation, and benefit packages, and dealing with local tax and legal liabilities.

Many corporations also have training departments to develop the professional skills and leadership abilities—including the "soft" personal and interpersonal competencies—of the work force. *Training and Development* magazine publishes an annual review of the percentage of a corporate worth that is spent on training and development activities, and in almost no case is this a small investment.

If we assume for a moment that international organizations provide these services—these competencies—not out of corporate benevolence, but rather because the services are a response to corporate experience that suggests that overall mission effectiveness requires these investments. The Employee Relocation Council, an international industry organization involved in helping companies move their staff around, does a thriving business in organizing conferences and trade fairs based simply on the idea that organizations need to develop competence in moving their employees around the planet. An industry has emerged to cover the range of services involved in successful expatriations, inpatriations, and repatriations—shipping people out, getting them into another country and culture, and returning them home.

According to recent industry estimates, sending an employee, his or her spouse, and their two children overseas can cost almost a million dollars per year. Hard to believe? Imagine your company wants to rent a nice apartment suitable for entertaining guests for you in Seoul or Tokyo. The rent alone can reach that figure. The cost of a failed assignment—or curtailment—for any number of reasons is quite considerable in dollars, but it might have a truly dire consequence in terms of the organization's mission. And what about the costs to the individuals involved?

Michael Fay, an American student at the Singapore International School, was caught vandalizing and defacing cars in 1994 and sentenced to caning. That the situation developed into an international incident, with the president of the United States weighing in and negotiating on the number of caning strokes young Michael should receive, in a country and culture as face conscious as Singapore, serves as a bleak testimony to the mission costs of failure. The Singaporeans were embarrassed and put into a difficult, if not humiliating spot, as was the U.S. government. Would another day's worth of cross-cultural training have been worth the expense? And how would the young Mr. Fay estimate the value of predeparture training that would have led him to better understand the consequences of a juvenile prank in that city-state?

Considering the Model from a Sojourner's Viewpoint

Let's say the 17-year old son of a suburban American family has an opportunity to go on a three-week summer excursion to Sri Lanka. What calculus will the family use to decide whether the trip is worth it, and if it is, how will they prepare themselves for their son's sojourn? The first step for the parents is to understand why this would be a worthwhile educational adventure to fund. What will their son get out of it? What lasting value would be derived that would make the risk and expense of the trip seem reasonable? Their reasoning, in all likelihood, will be quite a bit different from their son's. If the son is clever, though, he will present the trip to them in terms of probably somewhat exaggerated educational goals, personal growth, international and intercultural experience, and so forth. The son's actual goals may be more in line with the predictable needs of a teenaged U.S. American young man—adventure, the possibility of romance, the excitement of difference, the assumption of the social capital of doing something cool, and the important assertion of independence (forget, for the moment, the reality of who is actually paying for the trip.)

The parents' first critical task is to determine whether their son has developed the necessary personal and interpersonal skills—the emotional intelligence, judgment, and communicative ability—to benefit from the trip and not get himself into trouble. This is essentially the same prerequisite step that successful corporations and organizations go through in selecting people to expatriate. The assumption here, as is the case in organizational contexts, is that the prospective sojourner fully believes in his readiness for the journey. In my many years of selecting and processing people for overseas assignments, I have seen few people come to the mature conclusion that they are just not ready for the trip at that time in their lives. Most of us will deny even obvious evidence to the contrary when our hearts are set and our excitement is stirred by the prospect of an international adventure.

Having skillfully played his "educational opportunity of a lifetime" cards, the son has talked the parents into consenting to and funding the trip. Now the thrust becomes finding out as much as possible about the details of the trip, the security situation, the visa and passport requirements, flight schedules and ticket arrangements, and the myriad logistic details of the trip. New luggage—most likely a backpack—is hunted down at a recreational outlet (and it doesn't matter that no part of the itinerary involves trekking in Sri Lanka). Other vital purchases are made at book and map stores, clothing departments, and electronics departments—digital cameras and iPods are as indispensable for cross-cultural learning, evidently, as butterfly nets are for lepidopterists.

Thanks to the Internet and online bookstores, a Singhala language guide is just a few mouse clicks away. The cautious parents will insist on finding and talking to someone who has been to Sri Lanka recently, and perhaps will look at the U.S. State Department's website to see what it has to say about the safety and security of Americans in country.

What else should the family do? How will they know if the son is ready for an international excursion? How can they prepare for contingencies? What questions should they be asking? At this point, with the motivation questions answered, the family can start identifying the internal and external threats and assets in security awareness, cross-cultural competence, and personal/interpersonal skills. If, for example, the 17-year-old had recently demonstrated some lapses in personal judgment in the form of getting caught drinking a few beers with some buddies, now would be the time to go through a reiteration of the parents' expectations for their son's behavior in regard to alcohol—and resisting being pressured by peers—while on the trip. "You had an incident recently in which you made some poor decisions. We are trusting that you learned from that experience, and our permission for you to go on this trip is a demonstration of that trust. We expect you to honor our faith in you. That means that whether you have the opportunity to do so or not, you will choose not to drink alcohol, nor be talked into doing things you know to be wrong because your friends are doing them."

BEFORE YOU PACK YOUR BAGS

This discussion may have made you a little apprehensive but still eager to travel. When looking forward to some exciting adventure, it is natural to focus on the external assets and liabilities involved in the trip. What do you own or can you borrow or buy and bring with you that will help assure a great trip—or five-year excursion, if that's the case for you? What have you heard about the places you will visit, and the crime and health conditions you are likely to face? Much more important though is to look inward and come to some honest conclusions about the assets and liabilities that you are bringing with you because they are part of you (i.e., who you are and what experiences you've had). Now that you have a basic understanding of the Travel Wise Model, it's time to assess your personal and interpersonal skills, cross-cultural skills, security skills, and your motivation by taking the Travel Wise Personal Inventory in the next chapter.

CHAPTER 2

The Travel Wise
Personal Inventory

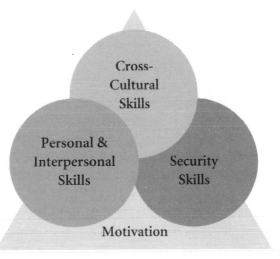

The threat profile that confronts you when you go overseas is a function of both external (country, travel mode, role, etc.) and internal factors. The internal factors are specific to you and include some elements that you can control as well as some that you cannot. To understand your threat profile, complete the following questions as honestly as you can. If you are uncomfortable answering a question, leave it blank. If you will be traveling overseas with someone—a friend, partner, or relative—you might want to share your answers and thoughts with them before you travel. At the very least, you should take note of and share some of your logistical answers. Try to develop an understanding of what your specific profile means about the threats you face when you go overseas. For example, you might want to consider how your gender affects your threat profile. Women, for instance, might be more at risk for sexual assault, but men might be more prone to simple assaults or fights. Go through this survey element by element and note points or questions you have as you ponder these factors.

PART I: PERSONAL AND INTERPERSONAL SKILLS

Personal Characteristics

1. Gender: Male / Female

2. Age: ☐ ☐ ☐

3. Stature: Tiny / Small / Average / Large / Immense

4. Posture:

   Tend to slouch / Droopy shoulders / Average / Erect / Buckingham Palace Guard

5. Physical fitness:
   - ☐ I resent having to bend down to pick up my television's remote control
   - ☐ I minimize any activity that might make me sweat
   - ☐ I know I should do more exercise but am not worried about it
   - ☐ I know I should do more exercise and am concerned about it
   - ☐ I try to exercise regularly but am not regular about it
   - ☐ I exercise regularly
   - ☐ I am frequently involved in active, competitive sports

☐ I compete regularly in events such as marathons, triathlons, ironman/ironwoman meets, or the Tour de France

6. Appearance: Describe yourself as others in an international context might see you.

_____

_____

_____

_____

Physical Characteristics

7. Health:

☐ I have significant health problems that require ongoing attention

☐ I have some problems—usually manageable, but occasionally problematic

☐ I am of average health

☐ I am healthy

☐ I am ready for the international space colonization program

8. Medicine dependence:

☐ I take many daily prescriptions that I cannot live without

☐ I take daily medication that I cannot live without

☐ I take daily medications that I need but could go a day or two without

☐ I take a medication when I have a flare-up of a condition

☐ I rarely take any medications

☐ I don't take/rely on medicines

9. Mobility:
   - ☐ I am not ambulatory
   - ☐ I am wheelchair dependent
   - ☐ I use a walking aid
   - ☐ I can walk without problem but cannot run
   - ☐ I can walk without problem and run for short periods of time
   - ☐ I can walk and run fast without problem
   - ☐ Masai warriors look upon me with awe

10. Vision:
    - ☐ I am visually impaired/legally blind
    - ☐ I am dependent on eyeglasses or contact lenses—I can't see without them
    - ☐ I am dependent on eyeglasses or contacts but can get by for short periods without them
    - ☐ I use reading glasses and/or need to wear sunglasses in bright light settings
    - ☐ I don't need or use glasses
    - ☐ I have excellent regular and peripheral vision

11. Hearing:
    - ☐ I am hearing impaired/legally deaf
    - ☐ I am hearing impaired and rely on a hearing assistance device (hearing aid)
    - ☐ I have a slight hearing problem but can function without assistance
    - ☐ I can hear without problem
    - ☐ I have exceptional hearing

12. Voice:
    - ☐ I cannot speak without assistance (mute)
    - ☐ I can speak but have a soft voice or a speech impediment

□ I can speak and yell when I need to

□ My voice can stop locomotives

13. Nervous system vigilance:

□ I am very calm and can nod off easily if not active

□ People tell me it is hard to get my attention when I'm focused on something

□ I'm pretty much in the middle/average

□ I am easily startled

□ I tend to be nervous/excited/hypervigilant

Behavioral Patterns

14. Risk tolerance:

□ I love to take risks and accept dares

□ I engage in extreme sports (bungee jumping, rock climbing, etc.)

□ I can be talked into stretching my comfort zone and taking a risk

□ I am somewhat risk averse

□ I refuse to take unnecessary risks

15. Sex:

□ I am very sexually active with many different partners

□ I am sexually active occasionally with casual acquaintances

□ I am sexually active only with a person or people I know well

□ I am in a monogamous relationship or am sexually inactive

16. Companionship:

□ I am most comfortable when I am alone

☐ I am comfortable on my own but prefer to travel with a friend

☐ I am most comfortable when with others and won't travel or go out alone

17. Alcohol/drugs:

☐ I frequently use drugs or alcohol and experience inebriation/intoxication

☐ I have used drugs or alcohol and have been inebriated/intoxicated

☐ I use drugs or alcohol but avoid being inebriated/intoxicated

☐ I rarely use drugs or alcohol and am never inebriated/intoxicated

☐ I never use drugs or alcohol

18. Comfort with conflict:

☐ I am an "in-your-face" type of person and enjoy conflict

☐ I don't seek conflict, but never shy away from it

☐ I avoid conflict when possible

☐ I don't deal well with conflict

19. Driving skills:

☐ I have had no accidents and never use a safety belt

☐ I have had several accidents but rarely use a safety belt

☐ I have had several accidents and use a safety belt

☐ I have had an accident or two and use a safety belt

☐ I have never had an accident and always use a safety belt

☐ I don't drive

20. Have you experienced any number of stressful life circumstances that would tend to make you less resilient for the rigors of cross-cultural transition in the past year? (These might include the breakup of a significant relationship; death

of a parent, sibling, or close friend; life-threatening crisis; or a significant depression or stress breakdown.)

☐ Yes ☐ No

List of Stressors

_____

_____

_____

_____

Financial Situation

21. Do you have enough money to easily cover the anticipated expenses of the travel, plus some extra money for unanticipated costs?

☐ Yes ☐ No

22. How much money have you estimated you will need, based on an average daily expense?

Average daily expense ($ or Euros)_____

Total number of travel days expected _____

Total resources required ($ or Euros)_____

Total reserve funds available for unexpected expenses ($ or Euros)_____

23. Have you left a will and power of attorney for your assets, debts, and other accounts?

☐ Yes ☐ No

24. If you plan to live and work a good part of your career overseas, where will you retire? Will you have built up social security credit and retirement and pension equity along the way?

☐ Yes ☐ No

Logistical Situation

25. Do people depend on you for their personal, emotional, and/or financial support?

☐   Yes   ☐   No

26. Have you talked to your family members about their wishes and estates, should they pass away while you are overseas?

☐   Yes   ☐   No

27. Have you left instructions for your wishes to be enacted if you should die overseas, or become incapacitated and/or unable to make your wishes known (e.g., life support, organ donation)?

☐   Yes   ☐   No

28. Do you have a communication plan should an emergency arise either overseas or back at home?

☐   Yes   ☐   No

29. Have you made your peace and said your good-byes to those you love in the event you don't, for any reason, return?

☐   Yes   ☐   No

PART II: CROSS-CULTURAL SKILLS

30. Urban living experience:

☐ I have no or little experience living on my own in an urban environment

☐ I have limited experience living in an urban environment but feel comfortable

☐ I have experience living in an urban environment and feel competent to do so

☐ I have experience and feel competent to live in any city in the world (including Beirut, Nairobi, Port Moresby, Baghdad, etc.)

31. International/developing world living experience:

☐ I have never lived in a foreign country

☐ I have some experience living and traveling in foreign countries

☐ I have lived in a foreign country for more than a year

☐ I have lived in foreign and/or developing countries most or all my life (e.g., as a third-culture kid)

32. Language fluency:

☐ I speak only my own language

☐ I have studied one or more other languages but am not fluent

☐ I speak another language fluently

☐ I speak several unrelated languages fluently

33. If you are now single and are intending to go overseas, have you thought about the possibility and implications of marrying someone from another country, culture, and/or race on you, your family, your children, your in-laws, your career? What would that mean?

_____

_____

_____

_____

 **PART III: SECURITY SKILLS**

Experiential

34. Self-defense:

☐ I feel unable to protect myself from physical assault

☐ I feel marginally able to defend myself during a physical assault

- ☐ I feel able to protect myself
- ☐ I am a martial arts advisor to commando forces around the world

35. Experience with crime/assault:

- ☐ I have never been the victim of a crime
- ☐ I have survived a criminal assault, attack, or incident
- ☐ I have survived several criminal assaults, attacks, or incidents

36. Attitudes on safety (protection from accidents, hazards, mishaps, disasters):

- ☐ I don't think about my safety on a daily basis
- ☐ I think about my safety when I feel imperiled
- ☐ I think about my safety as I plan my day's activities
- ☐ My safety is a daily concern for me, and I base my personal planning on protecting it

37. Attitudes on security (protection from hostile acts):

- ☐ I don't think about my security on a daily basis
- ☐ I think about my security when I feel threatened
- ☐ I think about my security as I plan my day's activities
- ☐ My security is a daily concern for me, and I base my personal planning on it

38. Fire safety:

- ☐ I don't think about fire safety
- ☐ I try to remember to change the battery in my smoke detectors
- ☐ I change batteries and have thought through an escape plan for my dorm/apartment/home in the event of a fire
- ☐ I think about fire safety because I've experienced a fire

39. Attitude about police:

☐ I believe police are generally competent, honest, and trustworthy

☐ I believe most police are basically reliable

☐ I neither trust nor distrust police

☐ I tend to distrust police

☐ I think of police as ultimately untrustworthy, corrupt, and/or incompetent

40. Where would you be safer in your life? Where would you live longer?

_____

_____

_____

_____

_____

Logistical

41. Do you have medical insurance?

☐ Yes ☐ No

42. Have you checked to see if your medical insurance will cover you wherever you go overseas (e.g., declared war zone, disaster areas)?

☐ Yes ☐ No

43. Do you have emergency medical evacuation coverage?

☐ Yes ☐ No

44. Have you made a list or record of your possessions in storage?

☐ Yes ☐ No

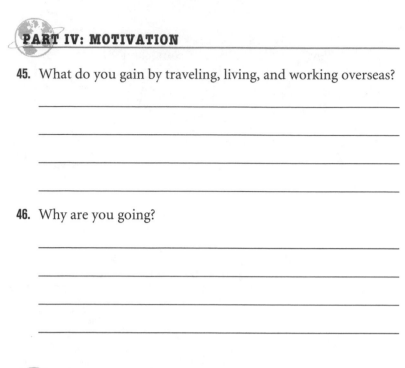

PART IV: MOTIVATION

45. What do you gain by traveling, living, and working overseas?

_____

_____

_____

_____

46. Why are you going?

_____

_____

_____

_____

BEFORE YOU TAKE THE PLUNGE

Now that you've completed your profile, you have much more in-formation to use in becoming a safe, savvy, and secure traveler. In the same way that cross-cultural studies start with understanding one's own culture, security awareness starts with an honest and unbiased look at who you are. The survey you've just completed is based on years of helping graduate students who were looking forward to international careers become grounded in one of the central competencies of *tradecraft* for an internationally mobile profession and lifestyle.

The range of questions might be surprising to some, but you are now aware of the range of topics to consider. You may be get-ting sick and tired of all this self-reflection and thinking, *"I just want to go!"* However, before you take off, take some time to think about what all of this means to you. How does it apply—or not—

to your planned travel? Knowing yourself—your capabilities, your limitations, and your expectations—is the cornerstone of your success in whatever international mission you embark upon.

Chapters 3 through 8 discuss these competency areas in more detail and will help prepare you to become a safe, savvy, and secure traveler. You can compare your survey results to some basic ideas about being a smart traveler and understand what your profile means. In some cases you can easily change from a less desirable to a more desirable answer with just a few simple behavioral changes. In other cases you cannot easily—or possibly—change your profile, but you can understand the security trade-offs that you make in going abroad and learn some strategies for mitigating parts of your profile that might be problematic. In yet other cases your answers might make you stop to reconsider your plans—or at least reevaluate the timing and conditions of your travels.

CHAPTER 3

Making Sense of Your Personal and Interpersonal Skills Profile

PERSONAL CHARACTERISTICS

It shouldn't be surprising that the survey's first questions are about your physical being. After all, your physical body is the one piece of baggage you will never leave behind. And just like luggage, each person has strengths and weaknesses: Big suitcases have enormous capacity but are bulky, hard to maneuver, and tend to be heavy; light nylon bags offer more flexibility and less weight at the expense of less security and protection than the hard, rigid shells of bigger cases. With some planning, though, and realistic expectations based on an awareness of strengths and limitations, you can make almost any suitcase—or physical body type—an effective travel pal.

Question 1: GENDER

How does your gender matter in international travel? Many of my students and clients over the years have bridled at the question. Gender differences in safe travel are not based on value judgments, stereotypes, or presumptions, but rather in a demonstrable, empirical reality. Either gender brings with it strengths and liabilities, and those realities vary in every country, culture, and sometimes even by arrival port within a country. Understanding and using those strengths, and actively being aware of and adapting to limit the undesirable impact of any liability, is part of security competence.

If we could conduct human experiments in travel, we could set up a marvelous set of controls and variables to test. Instead, let's take a quick imaginary voyage together and watch as two travelers, a man and a woman of comparable age, economic and professional status and experience, and personality type, both dressed in Western business attire, embark on business travel to two locations.

They leave from the same port of departure on the same plane and arrive at their first destination, a southern European capital. The customs and immigration officers at the port see the man as more of a threat than the woman. That's partially a male thing and partially based in the experiences of the officials—men tend to cause more problems and break more laws than women. That statistical probability, however, has nothing to do with our travelers— neither of them intend to break laws or cause trouble. But the male might well receive more scrutiny from the port officials. If his suitcases are opened and given anything more than the customary cursory check, his unlabeled bottle of prescription medications—two different types of pills and a daily vitamin—might well generate more interest and attention than the woman traveler's, whose bag is barely examined at all. On the other hand, the woman generates another kind of scrutiny from an admiring customs official: "How long will you be visiting?" (A more detailed discussion of gender and security appears in Chapter 7.) So the two generic travelers of different genders already have had different travel experiences. The level of comfort they have when entering the country will create an impression that will impact their respective learning and acculturation curves.

One of the best things travelers of either gender can do is to research gender roles in the cultures to which they will be traveling. How do women dress and act in the culture? How do men and women interact? Do men and women ever touch in public? Where are their eyes focusing when a man and a woman have a conversation in that culture? What courtesies are men expected to extend to women? How do men and women strangers interact compared to men and women who are part of the culture and are traveling together—perhaps married? How much personal space and distance is preserved between men and women compared to men interacting with men and women interacting with women in the target culture? Sometimes expectations of local men and women are different than what is expected from foreign men and women. Research begins with reading and asking questions before departing. It continues, however, and intensifies during travel and upon arrival in the target country and culture. Careful observation—even on a flight or train en route to your destination—can afford many clues to make note of, verify, and learn.

Careful observation, testing of assumptions, verifying and cross-checking with local cross-cultural informants and resources, and consciously trying and learning the new behavior will help protect your personal safety and security. Moreover, doing this will greatly catalyze your effectiveness in successfully completing your mission—whether it is business, education, pleasure travel, peace keeping, development work, or even fighting a war.

Question 2: **AGE**

Like gender, there is not much you can do about your age. In many cultures, people of advanced age are afforded a position of social prominence and accorded automatic respect, as well as engendering some degree of solicitous behavior from travel industry personnel and fellow travelers. In other cultures, however, age, and the inevitably slower pace and lessened physical stamina that comes with it, is regarded as a liability and is not always patiently tolerated. A 65-year-old woman traveling in New Delhi has a very different experience than the same woman traveling in New York City.

Similarly, at the other end of the age spectrum, the very young provoke a culturally based response that can either add to or limit the difficulty and danger faced. For example, one of my daughters was born in Bangkok. Thai people approach and interact with infants with warmth and delight. Cab drivers, hotel personnel, hospital workers, airline pilots and crew members, and—this is particularly illustrative—restaurant workers including chefs and wait staff seemed to take the presence of an infant as a sign of terrific good luck and joy. It was not at all uncommon to be eating in a restaurant anywhere in Thailand and have the baby swooped up and carried off by someone with a great deal of goo-gooing and theatrics—and not uncommon for the infant to wind up in the kitchen for a first-hand look at how that amazing cuisine is produced.

By comparison, in many Western countries bringing a child into a restaurant or aboard an airplane is considered a transgression somewhere between a sin and a crime. The difference in behavior represents a completely different set of cultural assumptions about the relative status afforded to weaker members of society. The same child crying can provoke outright anger and hostility in one scenario and invigorate concern and group efforts to cheer the child up in the other.

So how does age impact security? A colleague who spent his life studying airliner hijackings told me he had spent much of his career believing that hijackers generally release women and children and the elderly and infirm from hijacked aircraft because of universally shared values of protecting more vulnerable members of human society. However, in his later years he came to believe that the special treatment afforded the young and old by hijackers had nothing to do with shared humanity; it was simply far more difficult to deal with the logistics of those populations—to keep them from dying before the sought-after negotiated deal could be transacted. In other words, the subpopulation of 15–60-year-old healthy males (and non-pregnant, non-nursing females) are the preferred targets of choice for most international hostage takers.

Question 3: STATURE

Why would your stature—your height and frame—affect your safety and security? Because criminals prefer targets who don't intimidate them. That isn't to say if you are a slight-framed person of less than average height you could or should do something to change that. You simply need to understand that you are more likely—man or woman—to be a target than that 330-pound fellow sitting in front of you on the flight. The advantage that you have, particularly if you are in economy-class seating, is that you will arrive after having had a fairly comfortable journey, whereas the 330-pound man will land and need to be unfolded and stretched back into life after having been compressed into a seat that is half his size.

Question 4: POSTURE

In 2002 a group of researchers in New Zealand did a study on victim selection and vulnerability to attack. How you physically comport yourself does make a big difference in your security. The group found that "easy-to-attack" and "difficult-to-attack" profiles could be established by simple kinematic research techniques. The harder-to-attack profiles included individuals who took longer strides, walked with a more energetic and brisker pace, and seemed to have more weight—regardless of actual weight or gender.

If you think of crime as a vocation and criminals as practitioners of the vocation of crime, one of the skills that they need to master is victim selection—rapid assessment based on any observable data. That skill has *survival* and *security* value for them. You should understand and use that skill against them by remembering to carry yourself with authority and energy. This is not to suggest that to stay secure you need to be a speed walker. Instead, make a conscious effort to put your shoulders back, lift your frame, and walk with vigor.

Question 5: PHYSICAL FITNESS

Being in shape has survival value for both personal safety and security. Being physically unfit increases the likelihood that you may be targeted by criminals. Think of people in your life and experience who exude a sense of fitness. It is not just obvious muscular development—fit people exhibit a posture, energy, and confidence that deter crime. Thieves, muggers, and rapists are deterred by the appearance of fitness. It is not a coincidence that most police forces in the world implement fitness regimens for their officers. Fat cops not only are a threat to their own health; they are not credible deterrents to crime and criminals.

The Arnold Schwarzeneggers, Jackie Chans, Olympians, and triathletes of the world make poor targets for crime. The reality is that few of us are in that good a condition, particularly after a transatlantic or transpacific flight. While it is clearly desirable and good for your longevity to be in the best shape you can be, the security advantage in being fit lies more in having an appearance of capability than in actually having great physical capacity. Criminals are less likely to target people who they perceive to be strong and healthy. Statistically, you are safer and more secure if you are in good health and fitness, so physical fitness is a security asset.

Fitness is also an obvious safety asset. Your health and ability to cope with the stress of travel make sojourning out into the world both safer and more enjoyable. If you are contemplating an extended and difficult journey or expatriation, your preparation time is wisely spent getting in the best shape you can get into. Get on a stationary bike while you read and research the culture you will be visiting. Cardiovascular exercise not only strengthens your heart and respiratory system, it also provides you with one of nature's best stress-management tools. It helps keep veins and arteries strong and resistant to the pressures of long flights and can also help you control your sleep and changes in your sleep cycle caused by crossing time zones. Moreover, being fit can help you maintain an alert, attentive, assertive status and demeanor when you do finally arrive at your destination—typically a time when travelers are most vulnerable.

If you don't fit the fitness profile of a triathlete, have only limited time to prepare for your sojourn and many demands on your time, or just aren't interested in or capable of investing time and energy in getting in better shape, you need to keep in mind that you are at higher safety and security risk and make decisions accordingly. Trekking to Machu Picchu in Peru or around Machupuchare in Nepal are ideas that probably should be carefully reconsidered. There is no shame—only wisdom—in understanding and acknowledging one's limits. "Thanks! I'd like to do that, but I'm afraid I'm not in good enough shape to try that on this trip." That is a Travel Wise response.

Question 6: APPEARANCE

Your race, skin color, hair length and style, clothing, jewelry, and other attributes that someone would be able to describe by looking at a picture of you also carry cultural messages and significance to the people into whose culture you are traveling. In many places in the world it *does* matter if your skin color reflects lineage from the peoples of Africa, Asia, the Caucasus, the Middle East, or other parts of the world. The more remote the destinations your travels take you, the less likely people there will be familiar dealing with people who do not look like they do. They may be frightened, intimidated, surprised, or mouth-open, eyes-widened in shock to see you. Those reactions to you can generate some fear and hostility on their part. Remember that you are the visitor. Give them the benefit of the doubt and a chance to get to know you. Listening, smiling, and culturally appropriate gestures—a handshake, a *namaste* greeting, an appropriate bow—will go a long way toward signaling, "I may look different, but I understand, respect, and agree to play by the rules of your culture." Whatever language skill you have can be used to build bridges. The more different you look from the people you will be visiting, the more it is incumbent on you to learn as much language as you can, particularly greetings, pleasantries, and words of thanks and apology. Additionally, from a safety and security perspective, knowing at the tip of your tongue words and expressions for getting assistance, such as *Help!*, *Fire!*, *Police!*, and *Stop him!*, constitutes a critical safety and security competence.

If you anticipate that your presence—whatever delightful being you are, whatever gender, race, color, size, and appearance—will be markedly different from that of the peoples you visit, you need to psychologically prepare yourself for their possible reaction to you. This is an interpersonal self-awareness skill that directly contributes to your cross-cultural competence and your safety and security. If you respond to the awkward shock or surprise of a host country person to your presence with hurt, anger, disgust, or disappointment, you will be limiting your own ability to be receptive to this new culture and its people.

If you feel those emotions well up within you, use the strength of your heart and spirit and the power of your mind to understand what is going on, and try to forgive and reconcile before you rush to judgment. That's the door to cross-cultural understanding, safety, security, and mission success. You are there as a visitor for a purpose, after all, and to accomplish that purpose you should expect that you will need to marshal your heart, soul, mind, and emotional intelligence to the challenge. It takes courage to deal with the rejection that you face as a stranger in a strange land, and that's partially why successful cross-cultural experiences are so satisfying.

PHYSICAL CHARACTERISTICS

Question 7: HEALTH

Chapter 6 discusses using Maslow's Hierarchy of Needs as a way to understand your own motivation for traveling, but one of the most immediate human needs is for health—food, water, air, and a functioning body to turn it into ongoing human life. Indeed, nothing will grab your attention faster than facing a life-threatening health situation. If, and I hope this is not the case, you are in a situation where your state of health is imperiling your life, and you are perhaps thinking of either seeking treatment abroad or spending the remainder of your life traveling and visiting friends, relatives, and important places in your life, you already clearly understand the priority of health as a human need.

Good health, of course, is a desired state for embarking on travel, expatriation, or a nomadic international lifestyle. Good health not only is the best starting point for maintaining your personal safety, but it also impacts your security, cross-cultural competence, and mission and influences your sense of self-confidence and psychological and social resilience. Your immune system is also a product of your country and culture, and in your travels it will be challenged with threats in the form of germs and viruses with which it has not developed a combative familiarity. Therefore, starting out in good health will help your immune system learn and master its new environment expeditiously. Even with good health and an unimpaired immune system, travelers can expect to be vulnerable to germs and viruses that may well result in upper respiratory infections—flus and colds as well as some intestinal problems, skin rashes, and other predictable maladies of exposure to a new set of pathologic creatures.

Starting out with impaired health simply means that you need to take your condition into account as you plan and execute your travels. Even people who consider themselves quite healthy given their ability to deal with a particular condition in their host countries can face serious challenges that will negatively impact their experience and success abroad. People with asthma, for example, who have developed confidence in their ability to maintain a completely comfortable and healthy lifestyle at home may find that the new challenges of pollution, differences in humidity, dust, and antigens in the air can provoke ongoing asthmatic responses that can become very serious and detract from the pleasure and opportunity for learning that the journey otherwise affords.

Mental health is another area to consider with objectivity and solid preparation. Individuals who are on medication for depression and other mood disorders, for example, should talk to their therapists and mental health professionals about their readiness to embark on a journey into another culture. There will be new and stressful demands in adjusting to a new country and culture, and these new circumstances may well provoke a bout of a condition that is otherwise controlled. You should discuss with your doctor your plan for how you will prepare, what resources will be available to you, and how you would deal with a flare-up of any kind. That's not weakness; it's just good judgment in dealing with a particular condition.

Question 8: MEDICINE DEPENDENCE

Reliance on medicine can jeopardize both your safety and security when traveling abroad. In general, you are less fettered by not being reliant on any prescription medication, inhalers, contact lens cleaners/solutions, salves, decongestants, or other pharmaceutical products. But being dependent on medications certainly need not become a showstopper for your travel plans. It is simply a matter of awareness. You need to understand that the medications you rely on might not be available locally—at any price. You will either have to arrange for an adequate supply—with some reserve for those unanticipated but nonetheless predictable travel interruptions—or understand that your travel plans need to be arranged so that you will return before your medications run out.

What would happen, for example, if your holiday vacation was disrupted by a natural event—a hurricane, earthquake, tsunami, or quarantine because of an outbreak of a SARS-like global virus? Your return might well be delayed for several days or perhaps even weeks beyond your control. Like suddenly understanding the life-giving value of having drinkable water, being without needed medications creates a lifelong appreciation for having an adequate supply available. Not having the medications you need is a life-threatening assault on your personal safety.

Your security, too, might be threatened by being dependent on medications when traveling. Coming through a customs port with a bag full of prescription medication can attract unwanted attention from border officials, who understandably try to protect their own countries from an influx of illicit and dangerous drugs. Keeping your medications in clearly labeled pharmacy bottles with current prescription information on the labels should help you get through most borders. In some cases, though, you are well-advised to bring a note from your doctor indicating your reliance on the specific medications you are carrying. Checking in advance with your own embassy and those of the countries to which you will travel will save lots of heartburn.

Similarly, for those whose personal approaches to health maintenance includes lots of exotic daily vitamins, coenzymes, and dietary supplements, it should be understood that carrying these products across borders may well generate some additional scrutiny.

For the intrepid who wind up visiting local pharmacies for medications, a couple of caveats are in order. Drugs may well be cheaper and, in some cases, available without prescription in countries you visit. But buying those products may endanger you through the different quality control and dosage regimes used internationally. Because of vastly different pricing controls, policies, and subsidies, drug prices vary greatly around the world, and this creates a market for fraudulent and counterfeit drugs. These bogus products can do more than deny you of needed potency in your medication; they may themselves contain harmful and impure substances. Furthermore, the bargain on a prescription drug bought over the counter in a country with less stringent pharmaceutical controls can become a customs issue for you when you return through your own country's customs controls: "*Twenty* bottles of Lipitor?"

Question 9: MOBILITY

In October of 1985, in one of the admittedly more bizarre events in modern history, four terrorists hijacked the Italian cruise ship the *Achille Lauro* and took the crew and passengers hostage, hoping to trade for the release of some imprisoned colleagues. They ordered the American and British passengers to lie down on the deck of the ship while they pressed their demands with the Egyptian government. Leon Klinghoffer, a wheelchair-bound American passenger, was separated from the group and murdered, his body and wheelchair thrown overboard. The press made much of Mr. Klinghoffer's religion as the reason for his being singled out. In fact, there were lots of people of the same religion onboard. Mr. Klinghoffer was most likely singled out because the terrorists didn't want to deal with the fact that he couldn't be herded like everyone else on the ship.

While most airlines can advise you on assistance available for passengers with special travel assistance needs, travelers who are not fully ambulatory must assume the responsibility for confirming that appropriate accommodations are available. You cannot assume that because ramps, walkways, and wheelchair-friendly restroom facilities are available in your own country, that they will be available universally.

For those who can walk but need assistance with, for example, a cane or walker, or for those whose walking ability is limited to short distances and/or a slow pace, traveling with a companion or assistant is highly recommended. Put yourself in the place of an airport thief or mugger. Since almost everyone needs to travel with passports, credit cards, cash, travelers checks, and other valuables, who would you choose to victimize? Someone who could resist and/or give chase, or someone who would clearly not be able to do so? There is no honor among thieves—those who are desperate to feed their families or their own addictions will choose the easiest target.

This question in the survey has an option that indicates that you may be looked upon with awe by Masai warriors—Kenyans whose physical endurance and ability to run amazing distances at extraordinary paces is the stuff of international legend. As with physical fitness in Question 5, your ability to run great distances is largely protective in terms of your personal security in that you probably appear healthy and strong. It is only in unusual circumstances, such as kidnappings, that your fitness has significant survival value.

Question 10: VISION

As is the case with age, some cultures afford much more respect to those who are blind or visually impaired than others. People who have learned to negotiate and thrive without vision have developed remarkable adaptive abilities, but they must take extra precautions when traveling. Many of the subtle but lifesaving skills developed by the blind will need to be relearned to some extent: Traffic and directional signals and cues that white-cane mobile individuals use need to be adjusted for traffic coming from the opposite side, streets and sidewalks may not have curbs or use different pavements, and certainly attitudes and awareness of the general population may differ. Will a vehicle automatically stop out of deference to a person who is crossing the street with a white cane, or will the driver take umbrage and start beeping the horn and cursing?

For those who routinely use contact lenses, be aware that travel to a new environment may well irritate your eyes. Be prepared for a lost or damaged set of contacts and bring spares, as well as solution and glasses. Given the difficultly travelers can encounter with liquids while going through security at some airports, carefully packing contact solutions into stowed luggage needs to become a habit.

Those with excellent regular and peripheral vision, of course, have a slight security advantage. Peripheral vision is a vital skill in surveillance detection, a competency that will be discussed in Chapter 7. It also means that you cannot be deprived of your sight and made vulnerable by someone, or something, knocking or pulling your glasses off of your face.

Question 11: HEARING

As is the case with sight, hearing is an ability that you have naturally, have through an adaptive device (hearing aid), or don't have. You can't do much to change your reality, but you can plan and prepare for travels with that awareness in mind. Language acquisition, of course, is more difficult, but not impossible, for the hearing impaired. Learning nonverbal signals, gestures, and cues becomes a more important secondary communication competency.

There are some circumstances in which a hearing impairment may afford a safety advantage. For example, in an earthquake, hearing-impaired individuals will more likely quickly interpret and respond to what is going on by understanding the vibration and tremors than hearing individuals, who may be confused by the cacophony of sounds (breaking glass, things falling and hitting the ground) that are the result of an earthquake. A second or two of awareness of what is really happening can be lifesaving. As with visually impaired individuals, though, those who have a hearing impairment need to actively relearn some basic survival and mobility skills in a new culture.

In general, good hearing is a security advantage, particularly in that it can afford warning for surreptitious entry into your hotel room, for example, while you are in the shower or bath. On a cross-cultural level, to the extent that hearing impairment may inhibit language learning and communication, it may make adaptation more complicated. On the other hand, while visiting relatives in Europe who spoke a language that I didn't, I found my strongest, quickest friendship was made with a hearing-impaired cousin. Perhaps it was because he understood what it is like to not be able to communicate freely with everyone else; perhaps he just had more skill in getting his thoughts across in simpler ways; or perhaps he just is an exceptionally friendly and empathetic individual; in any case, the goal of my trip—reconnecting with my relatives across cultures—was greatly facilitated by one person who happened to be hearing impaired.

Finally, with the global proliferation of cell phones and iPods, it is not uncommon to observe people in any part of the world denying themselves the value of their own hearing capacity as a safety and security asset. Like alcohol abuse (covered in Question 17), these devices can seem to create a totally mobile womb of comfort around the traveler. You can bring your friends and family everywhere with you through instant global communication, and you can enshroud yourself with your own culture through your MP3 player anywhere on earth. But why did your embark on this voyage in the first place?

Cell phones and portable music devices can be invaluable assets to travel when, for example, you are stuck on a long flight or train or bus ride and you are basically protected, have little real opportunity to interact with the culture, and will otherwise be bored. But when these devices become crutches to protect you from interacting with the culture, or when they make you more vulnerable to threats to your safety and security, you might want to remember to put the device securely away.

Question 12: VOICE

A simple safety and security adaptation for those who cannot speak is to carry a whistle with them at all times. A whistle has become an almost universal signal for attention and a sign that something is wrong—almost every culture is familiar with the enormous power that a soccer (football) referee has through his or her whistle. The action stops and people focus on the source of the whistle.

Other than that, having a loud voice can have some survival advantage for both safety and security, but for cross-cultural effectiveness, having a soft voice, excellent listening skills (which means not talking), and the ability to yell on the very rare occasion seems to be the most successful set of vocal attributes.

Question 13: NERVOUS SYSTEM VIGILANCE

Nervous system vigilance is related to alertness. A person can be too alert, and thereby live with an exaggerated sense of threat that will make cross-cultural learning more difficult. Being too alert can also complicate safety and security effectiveness by people overreacting and thereby responding inappropriately. People who can easily become too distracted or absorbed (suddenly reading one's national newspaper as though it was more important than ever, even though one is abroad and therefore has even less ability to control what is going on back home) might not notice a thief lifting their purse, wallet, or laptop at an airport coffee stand.

Those who are so calm that they can nod off during a 15-minute stopover at an airport or train station are also inviting trouble. Save your sleeping for the hotel, the middle of your flight, or when you are safely in your seat or compartment on your train or bus. Prep for the challenge of arrival or transition by getting washed, having some coffee, tea, or water, and forcing yourself to be alert and attentive.

Ideally, you are alert and vigilant enough that you are on your toes, so to speak, but not frightened or startled by the smallest of surprises.

BEHAVIORAL CHARACTERISTICS

Question 14: RISK TOLERANCE

Competence in risk-taking is an area that, for most people, comes somewhat naturally as a side effect of the aging process. Unfortunately, for those who are *chronologically challenged*—here I mean the young and restless—competence in determining appropriate risk is an experience-based skill. Certainly some tolerance of risk is required to travel in the first place. In general, people are safer and more secure staying at home than traveling, not because their homes are safer or inherently more secure, but because they themselves are more competent in mitigating threats and thereby minimizing risk in their own cultural milieus.

As mentioned in Chapter 1, there are people for whom risk is the *raison d'être*. People who journey to places like Iraq not for ideological or financial reasons but for the sheer thrill of it are risk addicts. Without a constant flow of adrenaline, they can't seem to find happiness. These people are beyond the scope of this book and, generally, eventually mature out of it or don't last long. They make so-so travelers and are uninsurable.

The middle-aged woman who is happiest bungee jumping, parachuting, or rock climbing understands well the risk and is not pursuing danger for its own sake, but for the personal challenge that is represented in overcoming the risk. These people are not careless. They are gamblers who do everything to stack the deck in their favor so that they can win the pot. From their perspective, they have a mission that necessitates some risk, and they are willing to bear it with the full knowledge that they might lose. These types of people make good travelers but bad insurance risks.

Those who are generally cautious but can be talked into stretching their comfort zones are not as in touch with the mission—their own motivation—as the bungee jumpers, so they are not, and cannot be, as clear on what the risk is. For the bungee jumper, the sense of accomplishment and identity validation that comes from an extreme but manageable danger makes the risk of losing her life worthwhile. For the more cautious who find themselves responding to social pressures ("I didn't want to look like a coward to my friends!") by engaging in danger, there is no similar sense of value in accomplishment. The risk is accepted as a way of avoiding or minimizing the perceived or anticipated social stigma attached to not taking a risk. These types of people tend to make so-so travelers and poor insurance risks.

The person who is somewhat risk averse will only take on risk when there is a clear (mission) value at stake. When encountering a potentially dangerous situation, this person does everything possible to minimize the threat, always conscious of the value of the mission weighed against the danger—risk awareness. This person makes a good traveler and a good insurance risk.

The person who avoids all unnecessary risks is too cautious to want to travel much in the first place. He recognizes that he is safer staying where he is, and in the absence of some absolutely compelling imperative to travel—perhaps the Martians have landed and are invading continent by continent—sees no reason to encounter danger. This person makes a poor traveler but a great insurance risk.

Question 15: SEX

In my dealings with tens of thousands of travelers in the 15–60-year-old subpopulation over the last 30 years, the management of sex and alcohol while traveling are the two areas that seem to most closely define the wise traveler. Alcohol and substance abuse will be covered later in the discussion of Question 17. The need for sex is both a fundamental biological drive and a symbolic statement of the need for inclusion and intimacy. It is an area that defines cross-cultural differences between peoples and cultures, even as it is one of the most common of universal human drives and experiences. The thought of sex is exciting; the thought of sex with an attractive, romantic local person who represents the target culture is even more exciting—talk about experiential learning!

The answer to the question about sexual behavior in the survey reflects the assumption that *current behavior in a similar circumstance is the best predictor of future behavior.* A person who currently is very active with many different partners in all likelihood will find a way to be active with multiple partners in another culture. So what's the problem with that? It becomes an issue for safety, security, and cross-cultural competence.

The safety issue should be obvious to even the most sexually liberated of readers. Having multiple partners in a foreign context means you have even less ability to understand or envision the enormous number of contacts all of those partners have included into your extended network. One person with HIV/AIDs and/or a sexually transmitted disease (STD) can impact your (and future partners') health safety in profound ways, and you may not ever even know who the infection came from. The only countermeasure to the exposure endured through multiple contacts is total commitment to safe sex, every time, with every partner.

The same holds for those who find themselves having sex with casual partners on occasion. The only difference is one of probability: The fewer the number of partners, the lower the statistical probability of exposure. And the same total commitment to safe sex every time with any partner holds.

In both of these cases, a concurrent security risk is endured. Because interpersonal relationships is an area of enormous complexity cross-culturally, misunderstandings are not only possible but are probable. The greater the number of contacts, the greater the probability that some cultural boundary of jealousy, crime, honor, or slighted love will be crossed and be translated into a direct personal threat. There are also legal, financial, and other implications, particularly if one of the liaisons results in a pregnancy. The rights of mothers and fathers are not universal, and generally some heartbreak can be predicted to attend a casual cross-cultural pregnancy. Furthermore, in countries like Saudi Arabia, adultery is punishable by death.[1] This is no laughing matter, and while the cultural view of adultery in some countries is one of almost absolute expectation, the shift in cultural attitudes about sex as you cross borders can put your life—or freedom—in jeopardy.

---

[1] This fact comes from the British Consul in Riyadh, Saudi Arabia website (*www. britishembassy.gov.uk; follow links to Saudi Arabia; British Embassy Riyadh; Travel Advice for Saudi Arabia*). Other important notes for those traveling to the Kingdom of Saudi Arabia include: The death penalty is frequently imposed on drug smugglers; murder and sexual immorality such as adultery also carry the death penalty; there is no parole for foreign nationals; no suspended sentences are given to foreigners.

From a security and safety perspective, the last two survey response choices are clearly preferable. Even those choices, of course, carry no guarantees.

For younger people, including students, the decision to have consensual sex is a very personal and private one. In no case should one's desire to learn about the culture be used against someone, nor should it be confused with willingness to try on the culture or be culturally sensitive. You can be totally cross-culturally competent without having sex with a local person. Conversely, having sex with a local doesn't give you any particular cultural insight. Being clear with yourself about who you are and what the mission of your travel is will help inform your decision making around sex.

Question 16: COMPANIONSHIP

The same assumption used in the discussion about sex, that *current behavior in a similar circumstance is the best predictor of future behavior*, underlies this question on the need for companionship abroad as well. If you are comfortable being alone in your own cultural context, there is no reason to believe you will not be comfortable being alone abroad.

For people who are used to intimate or close companionship, your needs and preferences will carry across whatever borders you are likely to cross. If you are accustomed to being in a close relationship and for whatever reason go overseas alone, feelings of loneliness can become overwhelming and lead to behavior that may endanger your safety, security, sense of self, relationships back home, and ability to feel comfortable and adapt to the target culture. This phenomenon, by the way, can happen regardless of age or gender, marital status, or travel experience. Senior diplomats, businesspeople, soldiers, scholars, intelligence and law enforcement officials, as well as students and international development volunteers and missionaries can all fall prey to a loneliness the depths of which few will ever feel in their own countries. What the individual does with those feelings forms a critical point in determining who will become a Travel Wise sojourner.

One especially emotionally intelligent couple described their process for preparing for their year-long separation. He was going to a very dangerous job in Iraq, and she would be left with their 15-month-old baby and 3-month-old infant to take care of. From the very start, they decided things together. She understood and supported his need to go. For someone in his line of work, his sense of self, identity, and integrity would be compromised if he didn't go. He also understood the pressures that would be on her—chronic worrying about his safety as well as the overwhelming demands of caring for an infant and a toddler. He told her, "If it ever gets to a point that you can't deal with it, you call me and tell me, and I'll be on the next thing moving back home. You say the word, and I'm coming home."

They talked about how they would communicate. In one of the bizarre artifacts of the war in Iraq, cell phones are everywhere. They called each other every day. "He told me everything. He told me when it was rough, when he was scared. I knew he was telling me everything and that made it easier for me. If I had ever thought he wasn't being honest, I just wouldn't have been able to deal with it. If he isn't honest about that, what else isn't he telling me?"

The couple planned their vacations together, agreeing in advance to ask their respective parents to take turns watching their children for the first few days of leave so they could have time to get to know each other again. They talked about how they would work together to repatriate the husband into the family after his deployment, and he gave her carte blanche to choose the location of his next professional assignment. They dealt with the loneliness of separation by understanding the emotional impact on each of them in advance and coming up with workable solutions to stay connected despite their physical separation.

Of course, finding companionship in another culture is an enticing part of the cross-cultural experience. A friend, partner, or lover can offer both the refreshing unpredictability of someone who grew up in a completely different cultural context, as well as a caring, cultural informant who can act as a Sherpa guide as the new culture is negotiated.

Getting into a serious cross-cultural relationship has its own issues, of course. There are two areas in particular that tend to surface between cultures that are often laden with unspoken, unstated, and nonetheless strongly held subterranean culture values. One has to do with crisis management and will be discussed in Chapter 7. The other is in child rearing and parenting.

Child rearing? Isn't that getting ahead of ourselves? For almost 20 years, I've had the opportunity to speak to countless incoming classes of United States Foreign Service Officers. These people tend to be very bright, capable, ambitious, well educated, and well traveled. About 40 percent come in married. The remaining 60 percent are single, and I ask them, on the first day of their embarkation into a lifestyle that is highly mobile, if they've thought of the implications of who they will marry and what that will mean. Statistically, at least a third of that group will marry someone from another country and culture. That means that they are entering into a cross-cultural marriage, with all its interesting and sometimes very challenging clashes of cultural practices, rites, mutual expectations, family obligations, dealings with in-laws (which is generally tricky ground in most cultures; across cultures, it can be amusing to no end), and of course, the most important responsibility most of us will ever face, bringing another human into being. This information generally elicits nervous giggles—so I ask the groups to envision bringing their spouses home to live with them in their home communities and ask what adaptations they will be asking their prospective spouses to make. I ask whose rules of parenting will be followed and how those decisions will sit with both sets of in-laws, who, of course, know the "right" way to parent.

We all have a strongly ingrained set of ideas of what parenting should be (and, unfortunately, in some cases, should not be) based on our experience as children. These lessons reside in a very deep corner of our cultural identity. The late cross-cultural psychologist and humanist Marshall Singer's work on perception and identity posited the notion that each of us are products of our own unique culture, which is a function of all of the sets of cultures of which we are a part—the family, the neighborhood, and various subcultures having to do with our identity; religion; skin color; gender; a vocational group—all in addition to national culture. One of the most strongly held set of values comes from the one's own family. When two families are joined in a marriage, the cross-cultural clash that ensues may well have much more to do with family-related issues like parenting than with national cultural issues.

If this talk of intimacy seems far afield from safety, security, personal and interpersonal competence, and cross-cultural awareness and motivation, look at the international section of your newspaper or talk with one of your nation's consular officers. Paternity, child custody, divorce, pension and financial rights, and child kidnapping by an estranged spouse form some of the messiest, most emotionally demanding, and legally challenging work that occurs in consulates and embassies of all nations around the world.

Question 17: ALCOHOL/DRUGS

In terms of travel safety and security, it is undeniable and irrefutable that you will be orders of magnitude safer if you completely avoid being inebriated or intoxicated. This isn't a moral position; it is one based on statistics and experience. While you might be quite safe and secure in your own culture getting loaded at a neighborhood pub and staggering home, you are not safe or secure, regardless of your physical stature, fitness, or sober competence in any other domain. The scams that are played upon the alcohol impaired, and the penalties for alcohol and drug abuse, vary greatly around the world, but getting drunk overseas is the behavior of a fool.

A young Peace Corps volunteer I was counseling in Poland after the Wall came down was telling me he considered his excessive drinking culturally acceptable because there were plenty of drunks walking around the streets of his town in broad daylight. I asked, "Do you think, then, the Poles invited you into this program as a means of importing more drunks into the country?"

Alcohol (or drug) abuse has been a feature in far too great a proportion of the tragedies that I have come across in the last 30 years of international work. Countless rape victims, unwanted pregnancies, traffic accidents, robberies, muggings, arrests and detentions, fights, assaults, murders, and overdoses are the result of one party or the other or both being under the influence of alcohol or another drug.

Part of the reason so many otherwise intelligent people get into trouble with alcohol use abroad is because alcohol works as a narcotic to lower anxiety. And part of entering and dealing with a new culture means exposing yourself to some stress and anxiety—you won't know how to behave, what to say, how to meet your own needs as a human being, student, or professional. So having a product available that in most countries is legal and easily obtained and very familiar—Heineken beer and Johnnie Walker whiskey in Hanoi taste amazingly similar to the way they taste at home, no matter where your home is—can reduce one's sense of unease, if only temporarily.

Because cross-cultural signals also are at play in the often delicate and subtle negotiation of interpersonal interest, attraction, repulsion, and avoidance, alcohol use can greatly complicate the threat matrix the traveler faces. Worse, even sound strategies for avoiding inebriation can fall victim to the inhibition-loosening effects of the drug—judgment continues to fail precipitously as alcohol takes hold. The single most effective strategy travelers can employ is to drink little or no alcohol. Unfortunately, in cultures where drinking plays a large role in the socialization process, making such a decision will not likely facilitate the building of bridges of cross-cultural communication and may even interfere with building trust. Nonetheless, minimizing alcohol use and totally avoiding inebriation are fundamental competencies of the wise traveler.

Moreover, alcohol generally makes people feel less awkward in difficult social circumstances, where, for example, the differences of language and culture can create a sense of intimidation and alienation. Having a drink relaxes the mind after it has spent the day processing many conscious and subconscious cultural differences in the execution of life. Being away from home and in an foreign culture can engender feelings of alienation and loneliness. The opportunity to meet and interact with people in a social setting is especially alluring, so that visiting a pub or bar can be very appealing to the traveler. For those less experienced with alcohol consumption, the dangers of suddenly trying to gain more experience against the backdrop of a foreign culture can be much more problematic. For those who cannot readily find alcohol in their lives back home, whether because of social, legal, religious, or parental strictures, the sudden opportunity to have unfettered access to alcohol can exacerbate lapses of otherwise sound judgment. This isn't a statement of morality; it is a simple recognition that few things can jeopardize the value of an overseas mission quicker than ill-advised alcohol overconsumption. An analysis of crime statistics from around the world bears out this assertion: People are in greater danger for their safety and security when alcohol use is involved.

In some cultures, the legal system is much more sympathetic to alcohol abuse and abusers. Reports from several countries around the world, for example, describe legal systems that accept as at least partially valid or exculpatory the excuse that "I was drunk" even in serious cases of abuse and sexual assault. While this is incomprehensible to many around the world, it is the responsibility of the wise traveler to understand how cultural values and ideas about alcohol use and abuse can impact his or her safety. If a legal system will not protect you if you are in a social environment—a bar or nightclub—where you are likely to encounter inebriated, foolish, or predatory locals, you need to understand the implications of your choice to frequent such places.

The abuse of alcohol can be just as dangerous to men as it is to women. American embassies around the world, for example, employ United States Marines to protect classified information. The Marines tend to be very young, although extremely well-trained and disciplined. It is in the context of having a couple too many beers at a local bar that a Marine can run into trouble. A group of local men, themselves drinking heavily, decide to express their displeasure at American foreign policy by taunting the young Marine a bit. Foreign policy insults become personal after a few comments, and the manhood of the Marine and the U.S. Marine Corps are called into question. Common sense would dictate that it would be foolish to fall into such a trap as to get involved with a bunch of drunken local people who greatly outnumber the Marine. Unfortunately, common sense walked out the door after the Marine's third beer. A brawl erupts and the Marine winds up badly beaten up, and considerable damage results to the bar. Who will the police blame? Who will pay for the damages?

Women, of course, are more likely to be the victims of rape than men. Alcohol use sabotages the two most important safety and security assets a person has: good judgment and a sense of intuition—an ability to sense danger and hostile intent. If a woman is trained in martial arts, boxing, or other personal defense schemes and is relying on that training to protect her in the event of an attack, alcohol abuse will not only take away the defense but will delude the woman to believe she is reasonably able to protect herself when she is not.

Although not as traumatic, the alcohol-influenced decision of a man or woman to willingly enter into intimacy with a local person can endanger both their safety and security. Any sex, protected or not, carries with it the risk of sexually transmitted disease, including HIV infection. Certainly protection helps, but it does not guarantee against the transmission of life-threatening pathogens. But beyond the medical consequences, the allure of sex abroad— where no one from your own support system back home need ever find out the details—can be so enticing that even sober, rational, experienced, responsible travel professionals can fall victim to poor decision making. Those who are younger, less experienced, or less emotionally mature are at even higher risk. A man who would never think of visiting a prostitute in Washington, D.C. goes on a business trip to Bangkok. Titillating stories stoke the imagination. Extraordinarily elegant and beautiful women abound. A bit of loneliness, cross-cultural unease, and curiosity inspire a trip to one of the "red light" districts of town. After several drinks, a sense of excitement and risk-taking is aroused. The man goes to a brothel and has sex with a prostitute—let's not guess her age. The door is opened to robbery, mugging, HIV/AIDS, other sexually transmitted diseases, blackmail, paternity charges, guilt, lying to his spouse and children, and the psychic and/or spiritual fall from grace that comes from knowing that he hasn't been true to himself and has compromised his integrity. But that would never happen, would it?

And neither worldliness nor highly refined personal security skills protect you from these simple threats. It is a surprisingly common occurrence at U.S. embassies around the world to have an intelligence or law enforcement officer show up at the consulate to get a stolen passport replaced.

"How was the passport lost?"

"I was mugged in a taxi cab."

"What else did you lose?"

"My wallet, my badge, my weapon, my money, my watch, my . . . ."

"How did it happen?"

"I met this woman at a bar . . . ."

There are rings and networks of prostitutes, thieves, and muggers all over the world who make a good living by taking advantage of "temporary fools"—those who know better but fall victim to the allure of possibly getting away with improper, but nonetheless desired, behavior. Who will ever know?

Question 18: COMFORT WITH CONFLICT

An individual's interaction style in dealing with conflict is a function of both personality and culture, and it tends to be fairly resistant to short-term change. Keeping in mind, however, the type of person you are in terms of how you deal with conflict can help you turn up or tone down your interaction style to something that might work better for you in cross-cultural contexts. The ability to gauge and respond appropriately to the emotional content of charged discussions can have an immediate impact on your security, increase your cross-cultural competence, and help you successfully reach your mission.

For some people, confrontation through face-to-face verbal argument is one of the great pleasures of life, to be sought out and brought to an art form. In the souks of the Middle East, active bargaining and negotiating over prices and values forms the backdrop against which tea and life can be more flavorfully enjoyed. Coming to the conclusion of a deal with Israelis can be maddening in that they seem to dread rather than look forward to the conclusion of negotiations and seem to try to find ways and issues to prolong any negotiation, lest an opportunity to haggle be lost. In other cultures, public haggling of that form would be considered a form of humiliation and constitute a mutual loss of face.

So, understanding your own preferred style of interaction with conflict—when one party wants one thing and the other wants another—gives you a great advantage as you set out to become effective in another cultural context.

In general, being aware of how a culture deals with conflict is a useful way to get started on your travels. What will you bargain for and what will you be expected to just accept? Finding a balance between who you are and what the culture expects becomes an ongoing series of adjustments and reminders. Striking a balance that is politely assertive and that is effective—that's the goal—at meeting your needs is part of the fun of interacting with another culture. It is what makes cross-cultural simulations, like R. Garry

Shirts' BaFá BaFá game so much fun for students and participants in intercultural training programs.

The failure to be assertive enough by avoiding conflict is self-limiting and unlikely to yield a successful mission outcome. Similarly, a too aggressive "in-your-face" approach will very likely engender hostility, may compromise your security, and is again unlikely to contribute to mission success.

Question 19: DRIVING SKILL

This survey question mixes attitudes about driving (whether you choose to wear your safety belt or not) with psychomotor skill (the actual operation of a vehicle) and experience (the number of accidents encountered). The leading cause of death in the U.S. foreign affairs community overseas is through motor vehicle accidents—as pedestrians, drivers, or passengers. Operating a motor vehicle presents an excellent opportunity to experiment with how cultures vary around the world. Traffic patterns, drivers' competence requirements, rules of the road, unspoken but widely accepted assumptions about proper and civil conduct on the roads, and even fundamental questions about who has priority on the roads—pedestrians, bigger cars/sport utility vehicles, rickshaws, bicycles, or cows—become questions that have an immediate impact on your safety and security.

Given the threat to safety (from accidents) and security (what happens after two vehicles collide can include violent interpersonal confrontations) that is posed by motor vehicles, the one certain statistically valid response is to pay special attention to wearing your seat belt.

If you intend to drive while traveling, some simple things to keep in mind are to check the rules of the road *before* you start driving, make sure you are adequately insured, know where you are going before you start driving, and drive defensively. If you intend to drive frequently and in different countries, it is a good idea to get an international driver's permit (www.aaa.com/vacation/idpf.html). Remember also that carjackings are on the rise globally and are becoming more violent around the world, and that rental cars and foreign drivers are frequently specifically targeted.

Question 20: EXPERIENCED STRESSFUL LIFE CIRCUMSTANCES?

We have all experienced stressful life events, and travel itself can be quite stressful too, as you cross into and negotiate a new culture or cultures. Being aware of, and being able to separate out, stress from pre-existing circumstances from stress due to the transition of places and peoples can help you deal with both. In fact, this ability is a sign of the first component of emotional intelligence: self-awareness.

Not all travel is inherently stressful. Going to the Riviera, the Caribbean, or the Costa del Sol for a holiday is partially a way of relieving stress, after all. Sometimes travel is used as a reward for getting through a stressful passage of life—a PhD program or a divorce, for example—and sometimes travel represents a badly needed escape from ongoing circumstances at home or in the work environment.

Here the question of the mission becomes critical: Why are you traveling? If it is to get away from the hurt of a failed relationship, the reality is that no matter where you go, the relationship is still failed. Yet sometimes the newness of travel can rekindle a spirit of adventure, independence, and resilience, and help the traveler put the past into the past. Being clear on your mission is a great way to start your trip and manage your stress. Redefining your mission from one of escaping pain from a relationship, for example, to one of regenerating your spirits, capacity, and enthusiasm for life is more than a semantic exercise. It shifts the focus of travel and redirects thinking, planning, expectations, and assumptions in a way that can pay terrifically rewarding dividends and can recharge your sense of self.

Traveling for business can be a chore or a gift, depending on your attitude and the stress you bring with you. I was on a long (they always are) trans-Pacific flight seated in the middle of two businessmen, both returning from sales trips to China. The fellow on my right was burned out and couldn't wait for the beverage service cart to bring him another dose of alcohol. The man on my left was from a small town in Arkansas. He was returning from his sixth trip to China and was still full of enthusiasm. His company sold chicken hatchery incubators, and although his sales mission was not successful this time, he was beaming with excitement about the parts of China he had just visited that he hadn't seen on his previous trips, "For a guy like me, from a farm, to get the chance to travel around the world is a dream come true!" The guy on my right was on his third dose, and hearing the enthusiasm of our other seatmate, he couldn't help but share some of his negativity and cultural observations—how nothing in China measured up to the standards he was used to in Toronto, Canada. Two guys with the same business mission, one of whom is self-actualizing and experiencing learning and growth opportunities, the other adding to his own stress and heading down a career path of alcohol dependency. In one case, travel is restorative; in the other, travel is toxic. What will travel be for you?

FINANCIAL CONSIDERATIONS

Question 21: DO YOU HAVE ENOUGH MONEY?

With automated teller machines (ATMs) blossoming in almost every corner of the planet, the need to take bundles of cash around has largely been obviated. An ATM card and/or an internationally accepted credit card and a small amount of travel cash are all you need. But having access to a line of credit to provide instant access to extra resources should an emergency or sudden need arise is an excellent idea. For those who will be traveling or living abroad for extended periods, Internet-based banking and automatic electronic withdrawal and payment are essential.

Question 22: HOW MUCH MONEY WILL YOU NEED?

How much should you plan to spend on an average day? That is part of the research you need to do up front. Colleagues have laughed over decisions they've made when they've been caught short—or stuck with way too much cash for their comfort. A friend who was traveling to do humanitarian assistance work with refugees left with nearly no cash, thinking there would be nothing she would need cash for in the camps where she would be working. As it turned out, she needed quite a lot of money on a daily basis and had to rely on the willingness of her compatriots to provide for her needs until she could make other arrangements. That's an uncomfortable situation to be in. Another colleague wound up in the International Zone in Baghdad with cash that he couldn't hide, store, or spend. In these cases, there aren't travel guides to use as references, of course, so the only reliable means of getting a handle on how much cash you might need on a daily basis is to talk to someone who is there now or who has just returned from where you will be traveling.

Question 23: HAVE YOU LEFT A WILL AND POWER OF ATTORNEY?

One of the cruelest twists of life to leave your loved ones, should you die overseas, is the hassle and surprise of your financial and legal affairs. Unpaid credit card balances, unpaid student or short-term loans, and other obligations are particularly unwanted at a time of both grieving and mind-numbing frustrations and expense in dealing with repatriating your remains.

Making both your wishes and financial realities known to those who might have to deal with your passing is the only ethical course of behavior, regardless of your age or status. Without specific instructions spelled out in a will, your government may help your grieving survivors decide what is to be done with your assets and property. Leaving a will and power of attorney is a simple thing to do and demonstrates responsible, emotionally mature behavior.

Question 24: WHERE WILL YOU RETIRE?

A friend of mine spent most of the last two decades traveling from country to country teaching English as a foreign language. Some contracts paid well, some not so well, but he had a terrific time of it. Unfortunately, it didn't occur to him that he should have been saving at least 10 percent (better 15 to 20 percent) of his salary every year into a retirement fund. The money he did save was being taxed as income and had no protection from his own raids when times called for a bit of extra levity in his travels. He was shocked to come back to the U.S. and learn that the social security benefits he would receive would be prorated against his U.S. earned income, of which he had almost none. He will be working much longer than he had thought.

LOGISTICAL CONSIDERATIONS

Question 25: DO PEOPLE DEPEND ON YOU FOR SUPPORT?

No man is an island, entire of itself . . . any man's death diminishes me, because I am involved in mankind; and therefore never send to know for whom the bell tolls; it tolls for thee.

John Donne, Meditation XVII

One of my clearest learnings from dealing with colleagues coming back from war zones is that, by and large, their spouses and partners who stayed behind during their deployments suffered at least as much—albeit a different kind of pain—as the war zone veterans.

The impact of chronic, rational worrying is poorly understood but greatly in evidence. Many people who have a loved one in harm's way, who are powerless to do anything about it, and who are unable to understand firsthand how much real danger their loved one is in, find themselves in a cycle of endless worrying and dread. Chronic worrying can lead to depression, sleep problems, weight gain or loss, and, through the unrelenting stress, a weakened immune system. Part of the dread is wrapped up in not being able to control invasive thoughts about what would happen if the loved one lost his or her life and the partner was left to fend for himself or herself, perhaps becoming a single parent and dealing with the grief and loss at the same time.

The lesson of that experience is that even if you are a totally independent actor, unfettered by marriages, children, or a long-term serious relationship, you are exposing those who love and care about you to various levels of stress by your decision to travel abroad. This doesn't mean a year in Provence or a week in the Bahamas, of course, but travels in which there is a perception—rationally based or not—of some kind of danger.

By having made a decision to travel, you have put those people who care about you—as a sibling, child, parent, partner, or close friend—and perhaps depend upon you for some level of support, either financial or social, in a position that puts that relationship or support in jeopardy.

Travelers who are part of a marriage or committed relationship who are unable to travel with their partners face another set of challenges. Whether the separation is due to expense, work, or other commitments of the stay-behind spouse, or because the situation in the destination country is too dangerous, unsettled, or austere, both individuals are in for some challenges. If the separation is of any lengthy duration—more than a month—personal support issues, finances, parenting (if children are involved), and other elements of life that the couple has grown to accomplish as partners will have to be resolved individually. Stresses on both partners may make fidelity in the relationship an issue as well.

These concerns need to be talked about before, during, and after the travel has taken place.

For longer separations, particularly when one partner has traveled to a high-threat environment, a number of reintegration issues are likely to surface. Both parties are likely to have unrealistic expectations for how easily things will pick up and continue just as they did before. The reality, however, is that after a long separation both parties have changed, grown, and adapted in different ways so that things will never go back exactly to the way they used to be. Also, both parties may experience a bit of an irritable edge—the partner who traveled may believe she has made all the sacrifices, perhaps put herself in harm's way, and deserves rest, care, and attention. The stay-behind partner has spent the duration of the separation taking care of business, being a single parent, and accomplishing all of the home maintenance chores alone. He may have spent a good bit of time worrying about the traveling spouse—*Is she alright? My Lord, what happens if she doesn't come back?*

The traveling spouse may feel closer kinship to others with whom she went through the expatriation experience—they know exactly what it was like without having to spell out every detail. This can engender jealousy and a sense of separation on the part of the stay-behind spouse, who is caught wondering how much he should ask about her experiences, and when he should ask.

Patience in renegotiating these relationships is vital. If infidelity has been an issue, it needs to be brought into the open and discussed. A marriage counselor or therapist can be critical in helping the couple reestablish their mutual commitment and love for each other. Instead of looking to restore things to the way they used to be, the couple should work together to synthesize a new relationship and create a new way of being happy together. If he used to do all the finances before he went overseas and now she has taken over the checkbook, it is unrealistic to expect that the situation will revert to its former status. A new agreement on how to share the chores—and joys—of life needs to be worked out.

Question 26: HAVE YOU TALKED WITH FAMILY MEMBERS ABOUT THEIR WISHES?

This is obviously a sensitive topic that varies greatly for each individual and family. Having witnessed many expatriate friends and colleagues who have had to deal with the loss of a loved one while away from home, and having experienced the loss of a parent while living abroad, I know how a brief, frank conversation before departing can be really helpful in the aftermath of a personal tragedy. Should you experience the loss of a loved one while abroad, and you have either shared or primary responsibility for seeing that your loved one's wishes are carried out and the estate settled, you will already be behind the curve because of the time it will take to arrange a trip back home. You may also be arriving into a grim emotional environment, tired from your return travel, emotionally wrought, and going through the stages of grief and loss. Having a clear sense of what your loved one wanted and where important papers and information are can be a source of some strength and purpose in an otherwise confusing and difficult time.

Question 27: HAVE YOU LEFT INSTRUCTIONS ABOUT YOUR WISHES?

Again, although denial of one's own mortality has some healthy aspects associated with it, it isn't the best strategy for those who survive you. Leaving a sealed envelope with a family member or trusted friend can reduce lots of ambiguity and anxiety if you should pass away while abroad. It takes 10 minutes of your time, and can save hours—and even days—of agony for those who care about you and who will deal with the logistics of your passing.

Question 28: DO YOU HAVE AN EMERGENCY COMMUNICATION PLAN?

Having a reasonably accurate and detailed itinerary and a redundant communication plan are essential for going abroad, unless absolutely no one else on earth cares one whit about your safety, happiness, or well-being. In that case, you should still check in with your embassy. For a young person who has the rare opportunity to travel extensively throughout some part of the world, lots of available time, the ability to travel inexpensively, and adequate resources to last for some extended period of time, an itinerary might be a vague set of destinations that "seem interesting" written on the back of an envelope. In this day of global Internet access, e-mail can cheaply and reliably update family and friends on even the most spontaneous of plans. The point is, someone has to know where you are and where you are intending to go. This is not only a safety and security imperative; it is a vital element of your own ability to be contacted should an emergency happen back at home. Establishing a regular day of the week for an e-mail update is a simple solution for the nomadic and spontaneous traveler.

A redundant communication plan incorporates a reliable initial communication plan, perhaps a weekly e-mail or cell phone call, and adds at least one secondary means of communicating with a traveler. That might be by checking in with your embassy/consulate overseas, sending postcards or letters, relying on hosts or friends to serve as a communication liaison should the need arise, or making arrangements at a hotel, club, hostel, or place of business. As you will see in Chapter 7, one of the most predictable elements of a crisis is the failure of the primary communication system.

Many nations allow their citizens to check in with their embassies in foreign countries simply by sending an e-mail to the consular section. By doing so, in the event of an emergency you will have registered with the most important resource that is likely to be available to you, barring close personal friends or family in the country. Even if your embassy requires you to appear in person at the consulate or chancery, your time will be very well spent doing so. In the event of a natural disaster, for example, there may be no way to track you down other than through the information you left at the embassy.

Question 29: HAVE YOU MADE YOUR PEACE AND SAID YOUR GOOD-BYES?

"Why wouldn't I come back?" There are always a few students in my classes who, with the full and empowering invincibility of being in their twenties, look at me with incredulity. But people don't come home for a variety of reasons, chief among them is that some people die while they are traveling. That's a gruesome thought, of course, and seems so improbable that students, in particular, will ask, "What does this have to do with safety and security?"

For the sake of this discussion, let's say that a young person who has successfully made it through many of the perils of his own culture, including being badgered by parents about his grades in school, his clothes, his music, his hair, his friends, and his habits, has decided to spend his third year of university studies abroad. Although the parents are still funding the young man's education and travels, they are mutually at odds with each other and have trouble finding common ground past the cycle of criticisms, angry responses, and mutual intrafamily misunderstanding.

The young man dies in a car crash as he and some of his host-country college buddies went over the edge in terms of drinking in celebration of some recently completed exams. This young man never intended to break his mother's heart. He never intended to leave his father permanently estranged and forever regretful. He couldn't see eye-to-eye with them, but he certainly didn't hate them. He had no desire to torment them for the rest of their lives.

But without having made peace, without exchanging the emotionally intelligent—albeit demanding—work of saying, "Whatever happens, I love you and I always will. Thanks for letting me do this," he has, in fact, contributed to the lifelong misery of his parents. However, parents do sometimes lose young people. It is an unfair and cruel disruption to the natural order of things—parents should pass before children, after all—but to lose a child on these terms, without having at least temporarily reconciled, is to suffer the eternal agony of *what-ifs* or *I-wish-I-would-haves*. Any loss of this magnitude is painful, to be sure, but for survivors the thought that their loved one passed while doing what they wanted to do, with their mutual love and support reaffirmed and assured, is a far easier path to endure than the road of being plagued by self-doubt, guilt, and remorse in addition to the devastating sense of loss and grief.

What would you want your legacy to be if you—for whatever reason—should pass away while traveling? The psychological and emotional toll of unreconciled differences when someone dies abroad can add overwhelming agony to those left behind. Part of being an emotionally intelligent, savvy traveler is to understand the emotional impact of the "what-if" scenario and to do everything in one's power to mitigate the damage that would be caused by the consequences—inadvertent though they may be—of one's decisions.

On December 21, 1988, three days before Christmas Eve, a Pan Am 747 jetliner loaded with passengers traveling from England to the U.S. exploded in the skies over Lockerbie, Scotland as the result of a Libyan government terrorism plot. Aboard the plane were 37 young American students from Syracuse University and from the State University of New York at Oswego coming home for the holidays from their exchange student semesters in England. They had nothing to do with the Libyans and had no reason to believe that they would be the victims of an unconscionable, unrecoverable crime committed against them and their families. Those families were left to sort out not only the gruesome identification, legal, and financial challenges of repatriating the remains, but were left with the emotional baggage of their relationships with their children.

But it isn't only students who need to make peace with those who care about them and love them. Businesspeople and diplomats die overseas, too, as do soldiers and vacationers. And the circles of family and friends that surround those people need the protection of those travelers as well. A predeparture phone call to an estranged sibling, former spouse, or to Grandma in the Old Folks home can accomplish so much: It can safeguard the legacy of your relationship with that person, give yourself a benchmark for the relationship and a step back into it when you do—in all likelihood—return, help you to understand the solemnity and possible repercussions of your decision to go abroad, bring peace to your own soul, and get you to stretch your own emotional intelligence by accomplishing some difficult emotional work. But does this have anything to do with your safety, security, cross-cultural competence, personal and interpersonal skill, motivation, and mission? Of course it does—it has everything to do with travel competence.

A military colleague who was getting ready for deployment to a war zone told me how he tried to prepare for any eventuality. He and his wife talked through what would happen if he didn't come home. The couple had two school-aged children. They started listing the financial, logistical, and family challenges that she would confront as a widow and single parent. They realized those challenges would pale in comparison to the emotional stress she and the children would face. Even if he did return, the repatriation and reintegration back into normal family life after being in the adrenaline-soaked ugliness of war was not likely to be an easy chore.

They used some of their precious time before deployment to meet with a family mental health therapist that they all felt comfortable with—including the children. They figured that if the family needed help while the soldier was deployed, the other family members would have a relationship with someone who already knew them, already understood their issues, and with whom they felt comfortable. And, if the worst happened and the soldier wasn't coming home, they would have a built-in professional support structure to lean on while they dealt with the overwhelming grief and loss. Perhaps the actions of this amazing family are just an example of good contingency planning. It is also an example, though, of extreme emotional intelligence—not only being aware of the current sources of stress on the family, but clearheadedly predicting and planning for the emotional challenges of possible loss. Their actions were a profound gesture and reaffirmation of their love for each other.

If you haven't made your peace—reconciled—or just reaffirmed your love for those who love and care about you, going abroad gives you the gift of a great opportunity to do so.

CHAPTER 4

Personal Skills: Beyond the Basics

Travel is much like accomplishing a mission on the moon: You might have a pretty good idea of what the mission is, but you don't really know the terrain; you know you will have to improvise, but also recognize that there will be surprises. *You won't know everything you need to know.* For some, that fact represents a kind of torture; for others, it is the ultimate ecstasy of liberation. Whether the mission is business, pleasure, growth, education, career advancement, or romance, to accomplish your mission you need to have developed some personal and interpersonal skills. After all, if someone can't understand how to get along with others in his or her own culture, what realistic expectation is there that person would be effective in another cultural context, in which the rules are unknown, the language is a mystery, and everyone is dancing to the rhythm of a song the traveler can't hear? Chapter 3 hopefully provided some insight into your personal and interpersonal competencies for embarking on a sojourn. This section identifies and discusses specific skills and attributes that can make—or break—your mission.

Emotional Intelligence

Emotional intelligence consists of four component areas: self-awareness, self-management, social awareness, and relationship management. Each of these components is critical to the success of an international traveler, and several examples of people who exhibited profound emotional intelligence were cited earlier in this book.

Why start with emotional intelligence and not with regular intelligence—the IQ type of measurable mental capacity? Because I'm not sure there is any correlation whatsoever between intelligence and intercultural, international effectiveness or success. But I do believe there is a very strong correlation between success abroad and emotional intelligence. Why would that be the case?

People do not succeed or fail internationally based on their logic. They don't become effective through an impressive vocabulary (particularly in their own language). Nor do they deal and cope particularly effectively based on their general knowledge. People succeed when they are able to make the difficult transition to understanding life from another culture's point of view and interpolating a way to get their missions accomplished using a new set of rules. They are effective when they can sense, interpret, understand, and communicate the emotional needs and messages of those around them as well as their own. They become accomplished when they can deal with their own hurt, confusion, and disorientation not by dismissing or debasing the people and culture they are experiencing, but through getting in touch with what they are feeling and why, and using that awareness for new learning about themselves and the culture they are interacting within.

Self-awareness includes those attributes and traits that indicate a true understanding of self, and touches upon self-confidence, a healthy awareness of one's own limitations, being in touch with one's internal dialog and feelings, openness to feedback, and the ability to be honest with oneself. That these are vital skills for success in one's own culture seems self-evident; that they are even more important when working, visiting, or studying abroad becomes easy to understand when the challenges of effectiveness abroad are parsed. Imagine trying to learn the new rules for a very personal and involved game without the ability to recognize your own strengths and weaknesses; without confidence; unaware and out of touch with your own emotions; close-minded or defensive about receiving performance-related information on your behavior; and unable to honestly review success and failure, likes and dislikes, and the meaning of your day-to-day actions. Such a mindset would almost surely doom the most modest of international, intercultural missions.

The second component of emotional intelligence highlights the individual's ability to self-manage. Clearly, those who spend their days regretting something that they have said or done, dealing with unnecessary bad feelings that they have engendered or suffered, unable to focus and control their energies along desired and productive paths, and who have rued the loss of temper, fits of pique, and unintended interactions, have their challenges in life set before them. But taking these lapses of personal control into another culture can jeopardize safety, security, relationships, and ultimate success in direct and profound ways. The response of an individual to frustration, feelings of embarrassment, ineptitude, ridicule, laughter, and fear determine not only the personal effectiveness of a traveler to a new culture but also the attitude with which he or she will experience—and learn—the new culture. Self-management is a central cross-cultural skill that builds directly upon one's ability to understand oneself and correctly understand, interpret, and respond to rapidly arising, strong, and sometimes contradictory and confusing feelings.

The third area of emotional intelligence focuses on social awareness. This area encompasses those abilities that relate to the talent to correctly intuit, sense, perceive, and otherwise pick up on the emotional climate of those around the individual. It includes the empathetic ability to understand how others feel, even if those feelings are quite different from those that the individual is experiencing. The whole area of human intuition is predicated upon the ability to perceive the emotional states of others and to react appropriately. *Street sense* is often about perceiving the climate of unknown entities around the individual and "sensing" if something is wrong.

There should be no surprise that for the intercultural sojourner, social awareness is an invaluable talent as well as an accelerator and catalyst for intercultural learning. A psychologist colleague was interviewing me as a subject matter expert on what I thought was the single most important skill or attribute that separates successful expatriates from those who are not, and refused to accept more complex answers. In a word, *empathy* is as close as I could come to crystallizing the enormous range of the dynamic, interactive mix of skills, experience, knowledge, and attitude. Empathy is primarily a social awareness skill and is critical to bridge-building between the individual and the people and culture into which the individual travels. The whole idea of protocol is based on trying to make explicit, sometimes in a highly stylized or symbolic fashion, an awareness of hidden and unspoken emotional elements of a new culture. Diplomatic protocol is a primary example: More than anything else, it allows groups of individuals representing their own countries, cultures, and leaders to receive and share appropriate *respect* so as not to inadvertently offend peoples from other cultures. The United Nations would be a wild cacophony of fistfights and vulgar oaths without the imposition of rigid standards of protocol so that countries can focus energies on the resolution of differences of perspectives and ideas, instead of being mired in a cycle of retaliations for sometimes intended and sometimes unintended insults to the pride and sovereignty of respective nations.

The final component of emotional intelligence deals with relationship management, the ability to use one's own emotional awareness along with the awareness of the emotions of others to work in positive and constructive interpersonal modalities. This includes proficiency in group and team membership, and an ability to lead and galvanize groups toward the accomplishment of mutually desired outcomes. Try to bring to mind someone you know who seems to be able to get things done with people, a natural leader. Chances are that the person's relationship management scores would be very high. Now imagine how important those same skills would be in a cross-cultural environment. This person marries knowledge of her own emotional affect and simultaneous awareness of the emotional status of others, all in the pursuit of some desired end goal—the mission.

For a quick assessment of emotional intelligence, a number of self-scoring instruments are available both online and in training and psychological publications. Remember that whatever score and information comes out of an assessment, it neither guarantees nor precludes effectiveness in an intercultural environment, but the instrument can provide you with information about developing self-awareness and suggest some areas for you to work on and to pay particular attention to in cross-cultural settings.

Sense of Integrity and Honesty

An important attribute of the personally and interpersonally effective traveler is candor: a sense of integrity and honesty to oneself and to others. Without candor and honesty, an individual misperceives breakdowns in the travel experience to be the fault of others, *those people* in the new culture: Their routine processes take too long, are too inefficient, are wrong, don't make sense, or otherwise aren't up to standard. The reality is that for the traveler, there are new standards to learn, and failure to recognize and learn them is the failure of the traveler, not of the new culture, its standards, or its people. But this is a hard and challenging admission to make and to come to grips with at the same time so many new things are confronting the individual.

The ability to recognize and accept one's own shortcomings— understandable though they may be—is a sign of honesty and self-candor and is an attribute of the emotionally intelligent and successful traveler.

Sense of Humor

The related ability that perhaps is as useful as any other single skill is a sense of humor. Although this is an attribute that people either have or do not have, in jest I've advised people to go buy themselves a sense of humor before they go overseas. Most of us have at least some ability to see humor in our own mistakes and misfortunes and to have a laugh over them. The ability to laugh at oneself is not only a way of recognizing shortcomings but also of learning and dealing with the stress that those shortcomings would otherwise produce. People who have very high ego needs, who are insecure, or whose occupations or backgrounds tend to emphasize a sober, controlled response to everything tend to have a difficult time laughing at themselves. Others, of course, have a much better and easier time laughing at *them*, particularly as they get more and more backed into corners after they've committed some error of behavior or speech inconsistent with the new culture they are entering. All travelers make mistakes when crossing cultures. The choice becomes either to laugh along with others at the inevitable gaffs and intercultural faux pas that one commits or to become more disagreeable as others laugh.

If this seems impertinent, what happens in the aftermath of a cultural error followed by laughter is very serious indeed. While laughing at oneself tends to be remedial—it allows the individual to learn and move forward—when one endures laughter without the ability to laugh at oneself, the impact tends to embitter the traveler to the target culture. No one likes to be laughed at or to feel foolish, so for the insecure, high-ego, or overly sober traveler, the tendency is to take umbrage toward the new culture, a factor that predisposes the traveler to further errors and to self-limited or errant learning. Those tendencies can impact negatively on security, personal, and interpersonal skills, and have a deleterious impact on mission success as well. All this from the inability to laugh? Yes. In fact, if you don't have a sense of humor, and most importantly, an ability to laugh at yourself, *go get one!*

Sense of Empathy

As mentioned earlier, perhaps the most important human attribute to have for success in international, cross-cultural sojourns is a sense of empathy. Empathy is both a social awareness skill and, more basically, an existential premise: *We are all equal, and were I to be in your shoes, I might very well feel and respond entirely as you are feeling and behaving.* Fortunately, empathy is an attribute that can be developed, and some of the most satisfying experiences in intercultural work consist of seeing individuals—soldiers, Peace Corps volunteers, negotiators, students, businesspeople, and ambassadors—develop a greater empathy for those around them.

In fact, one of the most powerful intercultural learning simulations involves various versions of using the *culture contrast model*, brilliantly executed by intercultural legends Drs. Gary Weaver and Cajetan DeMello, both of American University in Washington, D.C. In their version, known as the "Khan Exercise," Dr. DeMello role-plays the part of a target-culture professional with whom an intrepid prospective cross-cultural sojourner tries to interact. Khan plays by his own set of rules and standards of behavior based, of course, on an anonymous culture. The student, hoping for success, tries harder and harder to resort to the rules, tools, and tricks of his or her own culture to move the business negotiation forward, which is exactly what pushes Khan further away. The perceptive and empathetic pick up on Khan's feelings of injured pride over the din of their own frustration and change their tactics. The vast majority of participants in the simulation, though, stampede right along with ever ruder and more strident behavior, determined to use an inappropriate solution in a new and different culture. It is only through Gary Weaver's skilled processing of the transaction that students begin to understand the emotions that were really the substrate of the negotiation and slowly begin to understand that the other person, from that other culture, is a real human being with predictable and understandable feelings based on what happened. Those who come to that emotionally intelligent conclusion are primed for further learning. Those who leave feeling that the Khan character is *wrong* are headed for a rough journey.

Assertiveness

While empathy is an attribute that builds bridges between cultures, positions, and peoples, assertiveness moves learning and interaction forward toward the mission. Assertiveness means being able to effectively push forward one's own agenda through persistent and appropriate means. It does not mean raising one's voice, yelling, insulting, or threatening, which are inappropriate behaviors in most cultures. Instead, in a cross-cultural setting it means being undeterred by miscues and differences in language and culture and getting one's needs met.

This probably seems so self-evident that it barely needs mentioning, but most failed missions abroad are more a matter of lack of appropriate, persistent assertion than failure due to safety or security issues, or inherent conflicts in desired outcomes. It can be intimidating to confront a new system in which everyone seems to know the rules—including the unspoken rules for queuing up at a service counter, for example—except the foreign traveler. But overcoming that intimidation and pushing forward to figure out how to get things done and meet one's own needs in a new environment is what cross-cultural learning is all about.

How can one measure appropriate self-assertion? Again, looking at the predictive value of similar behavior in a similar set of circumstance, those who are effective meeting their needs in their own cultures will likely find a way to meet their needs in a new environment. And that becomes a predictive element for mission success. After all, if an individual cannot meet his or her own needs in the home culture, how can he or she expect to meet needs in a culture that won't be understood and doesn't seem natural?

Ability to Give (and Receive) Feedback

Feedback is a basic self-learning tool that expands one's understanding of the difference between the intent and impact of one's behavior. Feedback is predicated upon the notion that individuals are not always able to bring their own assertive intentions into line with how others perceive them. Most of us have had experiences in our own cultures of intending an outcome through some statement or behavior, but the recipient or observers of the message behind the behavior come to a completely different conclusion about our motivations. "I didn't mean it like that!" is an all too familiar refrain.

Feedback allows individuals to cross-check the accuracy of their intentions against the perceptions of others. In its truest sense, feedback provides a mirror for the individual to see himself through the eyes of another. It asks the receiver of the communicative message—whether that is a statement or some action or behavior—what the impact of that message was on her. It is typically phrased in a structure such as, "When you _____ (description of statement or behavior), I felt _____ (nonevaluative description of emotional impact)."

For example, "When you put your arm on my shoulder, I felt really appreciated and part of the team," or "When you put your arm on my shoulder, I felt awkward and a bit frightened—I don't feel we know each other that well." In both cases, the goal is to let the initiator of the behavior understand the impact of his behavior and compare it to his intentions. Did he mean to make her feel awkward or frightened? Or did he want to demonstrate his gratitude, inclusion, and camaraderie? Perhaps it's neither of those. But the point is, he is now in possession of new and very valuable information about how his behavior comes across to at least one other person.

To be effective, feedback should be timely—as close in time to the incident, statement, or behavior as possible—but not in the immediate aftermath of a strongly felt feeling, for example, when the giver of the feedback is still feeling awkward or frightened—or mad! A dead giveaway here is when one is confronted by a spouse, partner, or colleague wagging his or her finger with a great deal of emotional energy, clearly riled up, and demanding, *I've got to give you some feedback.* It is clear that the person needs to talk to you, but what you will get from him or her has nothing to do with feedback. Like mirrors, givers of true feedback are rarely held hostage to a tirade of emotion. What you see in the mirror should be a dispassionate and careful view of another person's reality.

Feedback needs to be based on behavior or on statements actually made. Imagine, as the giver of feedback, that you are limited to conveying what a camera or tape recorder would record. Cameras and tape recorders don't include their own judgments or conclusions and try to reassert them as reality. Neither should you, as the giver of feedback; nor should you tolerate them as the receiver of feedback. By its nature, feedback should be something than can be cross-checked and verified by yet another person's perspective. It is a wonderful tool that should be used in a helpful, developmental way that incorporates the needs of both the giver and the receiver of the feedback.

Using this simple communication tool effectively can positively influence your relationships with people in your life, including your partner, children, parents, siblings, customers, clients, coworkers, supervisors, teammates, and students. It works best, of course, when it is solicited by those people in your life. But the clever and perceptive will benefit from a gently and carefully worded statement of feedback even when it hasn't been solicited. The trick, of course, is in knowing that if you feel a heart-pounding need to give someone feedback, it clearly isn't feedback that you are wanting to give. Nor should you fall into the trap of trying to use feedback for more than this very specific tying together of behavior and intent.

Within those constraints, the ability to benefit from, solicit, and give appropriate feedback is immeasurably valuable for the cross-cultural pioneer. If we sometimes have difficulty aligning our language and behavior with our intent in our own cultures, imagine how difficult it is to do so in another cultural context, even if we do have mastery of the language of that other culture.

Being able to find and develop a trusting feedback relationship with a reliable colleague from another culture allows the ability to markedly accelerate cross-cultural learning, better understand and deal with safety and security issues, and develop personal effectiveness and interpersonal relationships toward the successful outcome of the mission.

A simple example involves the true story an American ambassador's spouse, who arrived with her husband years ago to begin their tour in a southern African country. Wanting to dress fashionably, the attractive woman chose to wear a skirt that was far too short for the status she held in the new culture and for the occasion. To make matters worse, when the plane landed, the passengers disembarked onto a steep runway stair ramp, with a host of photographers at the bottom. The angle of the photographers worsened the perspective of the shots they took, with the result that the ambassador and spouse were the subject of a scandal almost upon arrival.

In general, it is difficult for even the best intentioned of host country nationals to share that sort of personal information with the spouse of an ambassador. However, there was a kindly soul in the international diplomatic community who, when given the chance, asked the spouse if she would be receptive to some feedback. "When you came down off that plane, I saw your skirt and more of your legs than I think you intended—and I found myself shocked and a little embarrassed." That was all that needed to be said, and the spouse got all the information she needed to realign her behavior—how she dressed—with the impact that she wanted: one of respect and propriety. This difficult but caring gesture helped rescue what could have been the beginning of a downward cycle of unintended messages and misunderstood responses about the culture and turn it into a learning opportunity—albeit a somewhat painful one.

INTERPRETING THE EMOTIONS AROUND YOU

Understanding and correctly interpreting the communications, behavior, and emotions of those around you, including perceiving the *affect*—the emotional content—is an important skill in the social-awareness component of emotional intelligence and has special significance in cross-cultural safety and security. Because the cues used to demonstrate and interpret emotional status tend to be culture specific, it is very easy to misunderstand and misinterpret the emotions of those from another culture. An awareness of the gestures and other nonverbal behavior of another culture greatly helps, of course, but tends to take some time and experience to master. Beyond that, those with malice and ill-intent will often not signal their true emotions to their targets. Being able to sense, intuit, interpret, and react to emotional states becomes a far more challenging proposition internationally.

A friend described to me an experience he had in a South American train station. He was somewhat on alert because the train station had a reputation as a place that was frequented by muggers and pickpockets. After buying his ticket, he was standing in a waiting area on the platform. Everything seemed normal, and there were no external signs of warning or danger. He said he suddenly sensed a wave of fear in others. He tried to remember what prompted that sensation—perhaps it was in the eyes of a couple of women who were with some children not far away on the platform. His alertness sprang up and he started noticing others, including some host countrymen, warily eyeing two young guys on the edge of the platform. One of the host countrymen made a split-second gesture, pointing to his eye and quickly looking at the two young guys. My friend interpreted that as a sign of danger—as a warning. He stayed on alert and began watching the two young men as they surveyed the crowd on the platform. They eventually focused their attention on a vacationing couple with one too many bags to watch after. After one of the young men created a momentary distraction, the other grabbed and disappeared with what looked like a laptop case—all in the blink of an eye. Had my friend not been in touch with that ability to perceive fear in those around him, it may well have been his laptop that was stolen.

Moreover, affect perception and clarification allows the traveler to come into contact with the culture in a way that helps unearth those elements of culture that are often otherwise invisible and unspoken—how the members of a culture feel about things. This ability, in turn, empowers the traveler to develop appropriate empathy and enrich interpersonal contacts and relationships.

Learning by Observing Others

The ability to observe and learn from careful observation is a hallmark of intelligence. This is the most economical and effective learning skill for those in a new and unfamiliar culture. Don't know how to buy a bus ticket? Watch others do it. Don't know how to behave with members of the opposite sex? Carefully observe others. Careful observation can be a full-time pursuit—there is always some behavior to watch, assuming you haven't locked yourself into your solitary hotel room. And even then, there are a million ways to learn about cultures.

David Kolb, a noted psychologist and researcher on learning, developed some useful theories on how people prefer to learn. Some people are abstract conceptualizers and prefer to think through their learning: *How would people in this culture exchange greetings?* Others are active experimenters and love to test and try out new behavior. Some are concrete experiencers and want someone to take them through a demonstration so they can get their hands on some new piece of learning and behavior. And then some learners' preferences tend toward reflective observation. They are those quiet and gifted people who can learn simply through careful observation. All four of Kolb's learning style preferences have advantages and utilities for intercultural learning, but the most economical preference tends to be that of reflective observers. They minimize their exposure to risk and maximize their opportunities for learning because they pay attention to behavior that is going on around them all of the time.

Listening Skills

Listening is essentially a form of aural observation, but in this sense it means listening for more than the words. It includes the vocal intonations and syntax, phrasing, accent nuances, and the color and spread of the vocabulary. Great language learners tend to be excellent listeners. They can master in an afternoon in a shopping bazaar what the rest of us would spend agonizing days and weeks struggling over. Forcing oneself to listen, in this very specific sense of the word, is a method for improving your language learning capacity. Careful listening also demonstrates respect for and determination to learn the target country's language and culture and is often associated with people of advanced intelligence.

Composure

Finally, success in meeting the mission of one's travel is greatly facilitated by a sense of composure and unflappability. *Things will go wrong; you will make mistakes.* What matters is how you recompose yourself, learn from your mistakes, and calmly move forward, with your motivation steadily affixed to accomplishing the mission of your travel. Being able to take setbacks in stride not only facilitates learning but helps reign in stress and emotional overreaction.

A psychologist friend described a kind of dysfunctional traveler he called an *awfulizer*. "Isn't it awful that the plane is delayed? I knew it would be!" These are people who make their travels eminently worse by their own negativity. "Doesn't it figure they lost our reservations?" These people suck the joy out of their own opportunities and poison the well for others. They are devoid of composure and unable to utilize the inevitable bits of unexpected life for their own gain—they don't have a Plan B, an alternative, in mind. Contrast the attitude of the person who was bitterly lamenting a flight delay with the person sitting next to him, who saw the time as a gift to finish reading a paperback she had started and then entered into a spirited conversation with another woman who was waiting for the same plane on the culture they were passing through. This is the same event, but a disaster for one person and a delight to the next. Which one are you? Who would you rather travel with? The ability to take unexpected surprises and setbacks in stride is vital to your learning, security, and mission.

So what attributes are not necessarily assets in effective travel? Those who are characterized as Type A—overly aggressive, take-no-prisoners, my-way-or-the-highway, and "I'm always right!" types—are disasters waiting to happen. Stay away from them if you are traveling. If you are one of these types, you have a great opportunity to recreate yourself by crossing over, stepping into a new culture, and trying on some new behavior.

CHAPTER 5

Making Sense of Your
Cross-Cultural Skills Profile

What is culture and why is learning the culture of the travel destination—as well as coming to an understanding of your own culture—vital to your security as a traveler? Does being effective mean giving up your own culture to some extent? Or does it make more sense to compromise somewhere in between the two cultures?

Developing cross-cultural competence begins with understanding the impact of your own cultures on your sense of identity, behavior, preferences, and perspective. But asking a person who has never interacted with another culture to describe his own culture is akin to asking a fish to describe what it is like to live in water. Even for those who have not traveled, however, there are daily opportunities to identify and examine differences in the various cultures of which we all are a part. It is through actively recognizing cultural variation as it manifests in society that we begin to be able to learn about our own culture—or more accurately, to learn about our own *cultures*. Traveling provides an opportunity for accelerated learning of cultural identity, for those who are willing to learn, and not judge.

EXPERIENTIAL

Question 30: URBAN LIVING EXPERIENCE

Experience living in urban settings in far-flung international locations serves as great preparation for intercultural effectiveness. You learn safety, survival, cross-cultural, and interpersonal skills— or you don't survive. The major feature of any urban environment is the increased interpersonal distance, often in spite of the greater proximity in actual living space. In a village community, almost everything is known about everyone; in urban settings, it is not uncommon to know almost nothing about the people next door. Without that sense of communal awareness, organization, and social reciprocity, you must pay greater attention to your safety and security, because no one else will feel much responsibility to do so on your behalf.

In most urban settings, the assumption is that the primary responsibility for personal safety and security rests with the individual. In fact, the presence of police forces, who rarely deter or interrupt crime in progress but serve to indirectly discourage criminal activity through investigation and apprehension after the fact, is a sociological development to deal with the lack of adherence to societal norms.

And why do people come to live in cities? People flock to the opportunity for trade, employment, education, and culture. But as development takes place around the world, large numbers of people are displaced from their traditional means of survival and they come to cities to find new means. Since there rarely are enough jobs, and many of those jobs that do exist are even more unpleasant than those remaining in villages, unemployed urban dwellers turn to crime to provide a means of survival.

Tourists and foreigners of all types make attractive targets. They have passports, money, valuables, and are not street savvy. Hence, for a traveler, learning to thrive and survive in New York

City helps to facilitate the acquisition of adaptation and survival skills in Johannesburg, New Delhi, London, and Bangkok. However, some cities are so dangerous for foreigners that travelers should really examine the value of the mission in terms of their lives. The list of the most dangerous cities on earth for travelers changes from year to year, but some perennial danger spots include Port Moresby (Papua New Guinea), Mogadishu (Somalia), Johannesburg (South Africa), Beirut (Lebanon), and Nairobi (Kenya). These have recently been joined by Baghdad and other cities in Iraq, and Kabul and other cities in Afghanistan. All these cities pose chronic, immediate, and serious safety and security threats to citizens within those cities; tourists and travelers can be expected to be at much higher risk.

This is not to suggest that those who are familiar with urban living won't have adjustments to make when transitioning to rural settings. Urban living experience generally provides more variation and exposure to a variety of lifestyles, economic strata, and difference and therefore requires more adaptation from individuals. People brought up in rural communities have plenty of variation to deal with but within narrower limits. In my experience, young people who come from suburban environments sometimes face the toughest challenges. The conformity that is the hallmark of suburban living with nearly identical, neatly trimmed lawns, and only so much variation tolerated in even superficial elements of housing and automobiles; exposure to individuals of a limited range or very similar economic strata—can all serve to predispose individuals to assume that their own way of living is somehow inherently more correct and desirable than the ways of others.

Question 31: INTERNATIONAL/DEVELOPING WORLD LIVING EXPERIENCE

As with urban living experience, life skills developed as the result of a highly mobile international lifestyle tend to facilitate adaptation to other environments—it should come as no surprise that *experience helps*. For those without much international living experience, candor in assessing that lack of experience can motivate spending more time preparing and researching.

For third-culture kids (TCKs), who are citizens of the world by growing up in different cities and communities as they accompanied their parents on a string of international assignments, their experience can be a double-edged sword. A young person can do quite well in a protected diplomatic enclave in Nairobi, say, but then get into some serious trouble returning in their twenties as a young, independent adult. In general, though, learning a sense of global street smarts at an early age is a significant safety and security advantage, and the cross-cultural exposure is one of the true advantages TCKs possess. Ironically, TCKs tend to have the most trouble getting along and feeling comfortable with young people from their "own" culture.

Question 32: LANGUAGE FLUENCY

Language learning is especially significant as the cornerstone of cross-cultural competence, and multiple language fluency is an invaluable tool to facilitate intercultural success. The very process of being able to choose from one of several languages through which to express a thought predisposes people to be able to think and learn from other cultural contexts and multiple points of view. Any given culture is simply one of several possible ways to meet the challenge of a people's survival. Similarly, language is a tool for the expression of thought. The more languages you have at your disposal, the more possibilities for exact and nuanced expression exist. Multiple language fluency has safety, security, interpersonal, cross-cultural, and mission value.

The requirements of the mission, whether a vacation, in-depth study, or negotiation, drive decisions about the extent to which language learning is necessary. In general, of course, mastery of some of the target language is critical, and learning more of the language is better. But language learning is an investment, just like paying for airfare, and should be analyzed using a rational set of decision parameters.

Often people rationalize, "Why should I bother? Everyone seems to speak at least some English here." Language mastery is more than just a convenient fluency in addressing needs and ideas; it is a tool for cross-cultural learning, a window through which to see the hidden values, assumptions, and thought processes of a community, and an inseparable part of understanding the people within the target culture. Is it possible to fully understand another people and culture without speaking their language? Perhaps it is, but only with extraordinary diligence and persistence. There are some concepts that are fundamental to a culture for which no appropriate translation exists. You can only approximate the concept until you understand the word in the context of the culture. For example, the Nepali word *dukkha* (sadness) means so much more than is available from a literal translation. It is as though the U.S. concept of "the blues," a similar, but different notion, could be adequately translated as *sadness*. The more you understand the language, the easier the culture becomes to understand.

That language learning and cross-cultural competence are strongly interdependent is becoming widely understood in the language training industry and the academic community. Particularly for cultures that share a common language, culture-specific language instruction becomes an essential component of the preparation of successful sojourners. French, for example, is spoken in several sub-Saharan, western African countries, including Togo, Benin, Senegal, Cote d'Ivoire, and Cameroon. French is also spoken in the Mediterranean coastal countries of Morocco and Tunisia. And, of course, French is spoken in France—and Canada. Each of these versions of the French language differs by accent, intonation, and usage. But culturally, these three usage areas are entirely different, so that for the traveler to Senegal, learning French from a Senegalese instructor has enormous advantages. Nonverbal language, that is, gestures, utterances, and body language, tend to vary by culture as well, so that learning French from a French-Canadian instructor is likely to be a disservice to the traveler heading to the wild vibrancy of life in Dakar.

If your mission demands an intimate understanding of the culture—development workers, for example—language fluency is critical. Indeed, it is unlikely that you will be able to complete your mission without fluency. If your mission needs are more casual in nature, or other parties either speak a language you speak or interpreters will be available, language fluency may well be too difficult and demanding a goal to reach. For the vacationer or pass-through traveler, the essentials of survival language—perhaps 100 words—should be the bare minimum. At a minimum, learn phrases to express greetings, thanks, apologies, good wishes, and as much vocabulary as you can to help you meet your basic needs, including words and phrases necessary for your security.

Keep in mind that any foreign language ability you have gives you power. It will enhance your credibility, augment your confidence and competence and may well prove to be a lifesaver in the event of a serious safety or security threat. If language learning has been an impossible challenge for you or an opportunity just hasn't presented itself, every moment you spend learning the language will pay dividends not just in your ability to express yourself and meet your needs in another culture, but it will bring confidence, satisfaction, an enhanced ability to understand the culture, and a deeper appreciation for the experience of entering into another culture.

Think of your travel as a special opportunity to learn some of the language of the people who you will visit. Given a choice of reading celebrity gossip and listening to the same old tunes from your own culture, or listening to language tapes and going over some phrases and basic grammar structures in a language book, push yourself to make the courageous choice, skip the gossip, and go for the language. There will always be another celebrity scandal or political tryst to read about.

Question 33: MARRYING SOMEONE FROM ANOTHER COUNTRY

There is a subpopulation of men and women in each culture who are fed up with men or women of their own culture and yearn for a different kind of mate—someone who has a set of values untainted by the worst of our own cultures. They are people in quest of a different set of choices, who want to change the rules of the game, and, by and large, understand that any choice for a companion from any culture brings with him or her a new set of tradeoffs between what is desired and what needs to be endured. And there are others who, traveling with eyes, minds, and hearts open to learning about a new culture, wind up falling in love with a member within that culture.

In either case, there are some predictable issues that test cross-cultural relationships. Dealing with in-laws and negotiating ideas about parenting, as mentioned in the discussion of survey Question 16, are examples. Additionally, the need for the couple to routinely engage in patient conversation, reflection, and thought on what is cultural and what is just the partner acting like a jerk forms a mainstay in successful relationships. Where will you spend the holidays? How will you negotiate varying levels of obligations to extended family members? Will you continue with separate religious practices, or will one or the other succumb to the subtle pressure to "conform" to the other's spiritual center? Which culture's evolving set of gender roles will most closely be followed in the relationship? What languages will your children speak and whose language will become their primary language? Which educational system do you want for your children, and hence, where will you live? Where will you retire? These are all questions that are laden with strongly held, subterranean cultural values, sometimes not even recognized by the holders thereof: *It has to be that way because that's the way it is supposed to be!*

Another frustration encountered by partners in cross-cultural relationships is the hurt they feel when one's partner is exposed to prejudice or narrow-mindedness from members of one's own culture, particularly so from family members. Your partner's culture or skin color is not an issue for you, but is the fact that it might cause others to react an issue for you? Will you feel embarrassed by your own culture, overly protective of your companion, angered at the parochial nature of other members of your own culture who haven't benefited from the mind-expanding opportunities of travel?

Any relationship is challenging, and cross-cultural relationships add a layer of complexity—if not difficulty—to the challenge. Understanding that there will be some issues, predicting what some of them are likely to be, and engaging in warm, patient dialogue with your companion that unearths hidden and unspoken values is the best immunization for the complexities of culture within a relationship.

LEARNING ABOUT CULTURES

To understand another culture and people, we first need to understand our own cultures and people: how weird, bizarre, unusual, and exceptional we are as representatives of our cultures. If a traveler can't comprehend that her behavior is a reflection of the eccentricities of the culture with which she has been inculcated, she is likely to assume that she doesn't have a culture at all—it's all those other people who have one. Without understanding that one's own culture is operant in ways both subtle and profound on the traveler, and that one's own culture is inherently ill-suited for effectiveness in the target country, subjective judgment takes place instead of learning. Instead of the experiential learning cycle feeding a continuous loop of newer and deeper insights, the cycle is aborted by inappropriate comparisons of how things are done at home.

But what is culture, anyway? In one way of looking at it, culture can be defined as the strategy and tactics a particular group of people use to survive in a particular place. A more academic description of culture could be a system of learned behavioral characteristics of most members of a particular group of people that is actively passed forward through generations. In essence, culture describes a group of people's way of being. It isn't *chosen* as much as developed and refined through Darwinian mechanisms—those groups that adapt well for their environments survive and propagate; those that do not adapt don't survive.

As a member of a culture, most of that culture's ideas and values are "taught" to us before we are even conscious of the idea of a culture. In Dutch interculturalist Geert Hofstede's metaphor, culture is the *software of the mind*. But if this software is the operating system that we share in a particular culture and it exists as the only operating system we have ever known, how do we understand what it is and how it differs from other, equally useful operating systems?

The Social Process of Learning about Culture

Cultural training, like security training, begins very early in the lives of all peoples around the world. The socialization of infants is both an indoctrination of culture and an intensive survival training course: We learn who is in the family and who is not; we learn what things we can put into our mouths and what things we cannot. The survival training—which, by the way, includes both safety and security competencies—has clear and immediate value. The intensive cultural training includes all the elements of culture, including appropriate behavior and unspoken values, assumptions, and ways of thinking. Most of this is done without a specific conscious or ongoing educational plan or program—parents just parent. And in the process, they introduce their children to their ideas about how people should live. Perhaps it isn't surprising that we rarely have time to include thoughts like, "Yes, this is how we have dinner and what we eat, but there are people in other cultures who do this part of life entirely differently." We learn how and when to say *please* and *thank you*, what to say after we sneeze, how to indicate it is time to go to the potty, and other culture-bound rituals associated with universal human needs. In other words, our parents become our primary cultural informants, and except in cases of cross-cultural relationships, parents rarely think about their roles as cultural Sherpas. They just go ahead and parent the best way they can, given the new demands on time, attention, energy, and vigilance that come with having a new human being in the home.

By the time young people start school, they already have been exposed to an enormous range of cultural training. The schools continue this indoctrination, of course, through culture-specific ways of teaching as well as exposure to content that further defines each culture: its literature, history, and sciences, arts, and assumptions about the physical body. Part of excelling and being rewarded in school involves conforming to cultural expectations for behavior and for acuity in learning its subcomponents. By the time young people are ready to venture out on their own to a new land, even as high school exchange students, they have already been completely exposed to, enmeshed in, and indoctrinated with their own cultures. Clearly, there is nothing wrong with that—the members of every culture impose their norms on their own people as a means of survival.

The downside of cultural indoctrination is that strongly held values will rarely be challenged by ideas from other cultural contexts. When young people go abroad, they not only have to deal with unlearning their own cultures and relearning cultural elements that will allow them to become effective in the new culture, they also have to deal with assaults on their values, their identities, and their very ways of being. In that context, when values are assailed, the common response is to get defensive and retrench in even more fervent belief in those values that are under assault. This is an understandable response, but not one that facilitates cross-cultural learning. And without rapid cross-cultural learning, the safety and security of the individual will come into jeopardy, as will the overall mission of the travel—it will only be a matter of time.

Of course, this response to the assault can be all the more counterproductive for more senior members of society who have not had the opportunity to live abroad. If young people are vested in their own sometimes poorly understood but strongly held values at the age of 15, the strength of those values generally increases with age, so that 25-year-olds and 55-year-olds may well find the conflict all the more troubling. This is, after all, why there is such a high value placed on exposing young people to other cultures as part of their education as early as is practicable.

Travelers young and old must understand that their culture is not the only "correct" way of doing things, but in fact only one of many, another example of which is manifest in the new culture. Furthermore, since by definition a culture develops for the survival of a particular people in a particular environment, the culture that the traveler brings is inherently *not* optimally suited for the new environment. In other words, contrary to the gut response of most first-time sojourners, not only is their own culture not the "correct" one to follow, it is the "wrong" culture for the new environment. That can be existentially disorienting, particularly when combined with the many changes in sights, smells, languages, and basic life practices that are encountered.

So, what does this mean for the wise traveler? It means that to learn about any target culture, the traveler must first learn about his or her own culture. It is only through understanding, for example, that the cultures of the United States, Australia, and Great Britain are anomalies—extreme in terms of the emphasis on the rights and priority of the individual compared to the other cultures on earth, which tend to afford more priority to the collective society than to the individual—that citizens of those countries begin to realize that their cultural biases are not universally shared. There isn't a right or wrong to this, of course. Because of the environments and histories of these peoples, their respective cultures grew to give much more weight to the individual than other cultures do. Those other cultures had equally compelling and rational reasons for giving more weight to the collective needs of the society.

Your Interest in the Target Culture

Learning about how and why cultures vary and how they can be measured and compared is part of the fascinating study of culture-generic, cross-cultural dynamics, and anthropology. For those who intend to have a life filled with experiences of crossing cultures, this is an invaluable area of study.

Most travelers, though, are consumed with the immediate needs of learning to become effective in a specific target culture. Their studies should also begin with their own cultures—initially focused not on how people in the target culture deal with life and business, but instead on how the travelers themselves deal with those issues in their own cultures. By adopting this approach to learning about culture, it is easier to understand and process the affective conflicts of values and practices.

A good (but unfortunately somewhat crude) example of this comes to mind from training foreigners to learn how to be effective in Nepal, in South Central Asia. Since the people I trained were unfamiliar with *charpis*—Asian toilets—and yet would be forced by necessity to use this type of facility, they needed to be "potty-trained" all over again. A charpi is an arrangement in which the individual squats over a fixture or hole in the ground to urinate and defecate, and uses water and one's left hand to clean oneself. The grimaces and revulsion that this topic brought forth from the participants reflected very strongly held, and yet unconscious, values around ideas of personal hygiene and sanitation that were drummed into those travelers at a very early age in their own cultures. Trying to start the lesson by explaining the use of the charpi would have encountered some stiff resistance and disbelief.

Instead, we began with a discussion, in excruciating detail, of how we were brought up in our own cultures to accomplish these basic human functions. We talked about the varieties, strengths, and shortcomings of toilet paper (quilted or unquilted; scented or not; tinted or not; absorbent or slick; one- or two-ply; 200, 500, or 1,000 sheets per roll); what one does when caught in a situation with no available toilet paper; what one does when there isn't sufficient water to flush a toilet; the fact that any paper tends to spread a viscous mess as much as clean it; and so on. After exhausting the conversation and getting people sensitized to the eccentricities of their own cultural preferences for dealing with this basic human function, the students were much more receptive to hearing about the charpi method. And yes, it is hard for many non-Asians to imagine themselves squatting for extended periods; adults rarely, if ever, squat in the U.S., for example. So to illustrate that it is, indeed, possible, I hopped up on a table in front of the class and demonstrated my simulated charpi behavior. Then I had them all practice squatting. While the psychomotor skills involved, squatting and using a limited amount of water to clean, are not all that difficult to learn, the attitudinal component of being willing to break with strongly held ideas of personal hygiene and adopt a new method that directly contradicted inviolable principles from the old culture was the real challenge. But this is how cross-cultural learning takes place.

Clearly, from the banal to the profound, there is a learning curve that the cross-cultural voyager must embrace. One of the litmus tests for cross-cultural success is the interest expressed by the traveler in learning the new culture. It is relatively easy to get good-quality background reading, research, and training materials for travel to any part of the globe from books and the Internet. But really digging into those materials, doing the research, and learning the language and culture still remain time-intensive and energy- and attention-demanding enterprises. Those who approach the task as an exciting challenge and learning opportunity tend to become much better learners and ultimately more effective in their destination countries.

There is no need to, nor should the goal be to, "go native." Instead, the intrinsic value of the target culture should be appreciated, inspire curiosity, and generate enthusiasm for learning, rather than inspiring vacuous comparisons. Those who can look forward to getting to know the ins and outs of a new culture without needing to evaluate its nuances against the prevailing practices in their own countries and cultures will do far better at objectively seeing the underlying reasons and assumptions that are at play. It is just as detrimental to do the opposite, though, and after having had brief exposure to a new culture and the way of life it represents, reject all of the values and behaviors of one's own culture in favor of those of the new culture.

A more balanced approach is to understand and appreciate the target culture as being entirely appropriate for that people and place, and enthusiastically learn about it without rejecting one's own culture and identity. This approach allows the traveler to develop a second set of life skills with which to interact, rather than holding on exclusively to the old, or categorically rejecting and replacing the old with the new.

Active Learning—Willingness to Try Target Culture Behavior

As illustrated in the charpi example earlier, not every moment of cross-cultural learning is filled with fun. Some learning is difficult and painful and sometimes demands that we first must disassemble cherished ideas, practices, and attitudes. It requires us to be in situations in which we may look and feel awkward, embarrassed, and foolish and thereby challenges our self-esteem, identity, and confidence. The willingness to embrace the challenge, take on the opportunity, and push oneself to become an active, aggressive learner separates those who will do well from those who most likely will not.

A close friend of mine, Mari, was arguably the worst language learner any of her language trainers in Nepal had ever encountered. She simply had no "ear"—the talent for hearing and being able to reproduce the sounds required in the pronunciation of the target language; didn't understand the structure; and was philosophically opposed to learning to use pre- and post-positional prepositions and other grammatical features of the language. What she did have, though, was an iron-clad determination to persevere, no matter how painful the expressions of those with whom she was trying to communicate, and no matter the peals of laughter from the children with whom she tried to practice her language. And practice she did. She would go and sit or work with women as they did their chores; she sat and listened endlessly to the elders of the community as they discussed the politics of the day; she played ball with the kids in the schoolyard; and she would go to the market stalls and tea shops just to practice her survival language skills. Her willingness to get out there and try her new language in every possible venue, exercising any skill or word she had been able to master, eventually paid off. She became quite proficient—and married a guy from the target culture. Mari is a posterchild for the approach one must take with learning a new language and culture.

THE BENEFITS OF YOUR CROSS-CULTURAL SKILLS

Cultural competence, including language fluency, impacts your safety and security. One of the most interesting areas of crisis management work is in understanding how crisis management ideas and attitudes vary cross-culturally. Security awareness consists of more than understanding the threat—it also includes understanding what resources are available within the culture to mitigate the threat. Understanding those resources—the police and the legal system, for example—can mean the difference between a situation that gets resolved and one that spirals downward. Language and cultural fluency are invaluable should a natural disaster or other unintended but nonetheless serious threat occur. The ability to communicate rapidly, accurately, and appropriately in the aftermath of a motor vehicle accident, for example, can mean the difference in getting lifesaving treatment or of receiving a blood transfusion from a blood supply that might be tainted with HIV.

Language and cultural fluency greatly facilitate interpersonal relationships, confidence, and competence in the target country. Being able to speak the language of your hosts demonstrates respect, and understanding appropriate behavior—beyond a simple list of "dos and don'ts"—affords an incredible advantage for the traveler. Perhaps less obvious are the benefits of personal skills afforded by cross-cultural competence. As your familiarity and comfort with the target country increases, your sense of self-esteem and resilience tend to grow as well. Slights, surprises, and hassles that would perplex and threaten less proficient travelers become predictable and even humorous, although unimportant, interruptions for the cross-culturally competent. Cross-cultural competence empowers composure and builds confidence.

Finally, language and cultural ability strengthen motivation in a number of ways. First, the sense of exhaustion and of being overwhelmed by a new culture is greatly reduced by fluency. (Make no mistake, though, speaking in another language, regardless of fluency, can be a very tiring activity. Speaking all day in another language, for example, as a teacher, can be exhausting—and literally drive the teacher to sleep, so that her mind can rest and recuperate.) Secondly, the investment in learning the target language and culture tends to strengthen the determination of the traveler to see things through to a successful outcome. Third, language and cultural mastery can change the identity of the traveler to someone who feels part of the new culture as well as the old and becomes able to be effective in either culture. Just as success tends to be intrinsically motivating, success in negotiating a new culture becomes fuel for further ambition and success.

Whatever personal or organizational mission brought the traveler to the new culture, language and cultural fluency will help empower success in mission accomplishment. Vacation travel is made more enjoyable and richer; scholarship and academic pursuits become both more achievable and more enriching and broadening; business goals become easier to navigate and negotiate, less bewildering, and more predictable; development work becomes more empathetic and sustainable; diplomatic goals become more achievable; and for those who travel in search of love, your chances of finding it are much improved if you understand what it means in another cultural context.

CHAPTER 6

Security Skills: Beyond the Basics

The very fact that humans generally quickly learn survival lessons in our own cultures from an early age complicates our efforts later in life to be safe—and effective—in other cultures. Sometimes we have to unlearn hard-won lessons of when and of what we should be afraid. Worse yet, since so many of the lessons we learn about safety and security have to do with correctly interpreting and responding appropriately to the emotional cues of others in our own cultures, when we go overseas, we are using a sixth sense—an ability to intuit and palpate danger—that is based on the wrong cultural set of learnings.

The most powerful protective shield available to an international travel is her basic safety and security awareness and competence. Similarly, as you will see in Chapter 9, the collective security awareness and competence of the workforce is any organization's best guarantee of freedom from unnecessary risk. Security competence is comprised of knowledge, travel skills, and an attitude that demonstrates a healthy and realistic respect for the various threats to safety and security. Awareness is realizing that, *Yes—it can happen to me! I must do everything I can to make sure it doesn't.*

Just having that awareness can change your risk profile immediately. As will be discussed in Chapter 8, *motivation influences behavior*. If the motivation to be safe and secure is always in the mind of the traveler, he is likely to behave in a way that protects his safety and security. Many of the general principles of travel safety and security (such as avoiding excessive drinking, unprotected or ill-advised sex, and motor vehicle accidents) have already been covered in Chapter 3. We will turn our attention to basic security skills, experience, and travel tradecraft—managing logistics—as the next parts of the Travel Wise Model.

Attention, Awareness, and Attitude

The "Triple-A" of international security competency encompasses a range of attributes of the traveler's attention, awareness, and attitude about his or her own safety and security. These attributes are developed through experience in life and travel by the competent and ignored or not yet developed by the others. The experientially derived attributes include self-confidence, surveillance detection, and threat identification and perception, which interact in powerful and protective ways. The following sections discuss these attributes.

Self-Confidence

Just as inattention to one's surroundings can be a dangerous liability, a sense of self-confidence founded on excellent preparation can create the tactical advantage necessary to remain safe and secure. Self-confidence means understanding that there are threats in the environment, thinking through those threats, and reaching a realistic assessment that those challenges can be managed. Self-confidence gives individuals a sense of empowerment and capability, and the posture and stride to deter criminal intent. It also engenders an emotional state in travelers that favors composure over panic and active, quick-witted response over freezing or becoming intimidated.

Self-confidence is, of course, facilitated by a number of experiences in one's life that demonstrate to the individual her own competency and skill at coping with the emotional trials and successfully managing whatever threat or challenge the environment poses. For the less experienced traveler, one way to get in touch with a sense of self-confidence is to candidly inventory the assets and liabilities that are part of the individual's reality (the survey in Chapter 2 is a good starting point for this). Having an awareness of those strengths and liabilities not only provides a basis for intelligent decision making in the event of some problem, but it can help you identify areas in which to focus your preparation.

Excessive self confidence, on the other hand, is probably more of a liability than the lack of self-confidence. When excessive confidence manifests as cockiness or an arrogant disregard for danger, it deceives the individual and fosters an attitude of insouciant indifference and inattention. This attitude involves an exaggerated denial of one's vulnerability and mortality. Cross-culturally, excessive self-confidence can come across as being rude and overbearing, attributes that won't encourage host country people to be helpful or to share in the responsibility for the individual's safety and security.

Surveillance Detection

The behavioral part of the sixth sense that author Gavin de Becker describes as the *gift of fear* includes the sometimes entirely subconscious skill of surveillance detection. This is a process of becoming aware that someone—or some group—is paying unusually close attention to an individual's presence, movements, conversations, or activities. Being able to pick up on a set of eyes focused on you within a crowd, or catching the slightest of glances and/or nuances of body language sometimes happens at a level that we are not consciously aware of but which we can feel nonetheless. "I could *feel* his eyes staring at me" or "I *felt* like I was being watched" are both reflections of tiny bits of behavioral data that the individual took in and analyzed without conscious effort or awareness.

Paying attention to those sometime vague perceptions or fleeting observations is a basic skill in surveillance detection. Bringing to the forefront of consciousness an alertness that allows one to actively scan the environment for surveillance is the mastery of that skill.

Surveillance detection is important because it robs those of malicious intent of one of their chief advantages—surprise. But beyond that, being alert and recognizing the potential situation can send a terrifying and unnerving message to the surveillants (those who engage in surveillance)—that they have been discovered. Security industry lore is filled with examples of surveillants being discovered and running scared, moving on to another target, or heading for the hills; this goes for petty criminals, hardened terrorists, and espionage agents. There is something quite intimidating, evidently, about being discovered—it's almost as though the perpetrator's sense of privacy has been violated!

There are times when one's conscious and heightened surveillance detection needs to be turned on proactively—precisely at those places where travelers and expatriates are most vulnerable: airports, train stations, shopping malls and markets, the drive to and from work, and other situations of relative exposure. Unfortunately, one of the side effects of alcohol and substance abuse is a diminished ability for acute observation and perception, which is another reason to practice moderation abroad. But for the sober person, tuning into one's surroundings includes visually scanning the environment, paying attention to being followed or tracked, whether on foot or in a car, and looking for those miniscule behavioral clues that indicate someone else's abnormal interest.

Any crime, other than a crime of spontaneous opportunity, requires some degree of surveillance. Being able to anticipate times and places of vulnerability puts the traveler or expatriate in control of her level of attentiveness. Law enforcement agencies teach a concept called Cooper's Colors or the Cooper Color Code. It defines four levels of vigilance and readiness by color: white, yellow, orange, and red. White corresponds to a level of total cognitive inattention. This level is appropriate only for places and times the individual feels and knows himself to be in a safe and protected environment, such as when relaxing in one's study or den or in a well-protected hotel room. It can be disastrous in situations in which any threat is possible, even unintended challenges to one's safety.

In Color Yellow, the individual is consciously but calmly vigilant, turning on his built-in surveillance detection mechanisms. The individual is aware that there may be threats in the environment and pays attention to potential sources of threat as an initial phase of mitigating any security or safety issue. In Color Orange, one senses a specific threat, becomes primed to respond, and is vigilant of sources of threat, including surveillance. In Color Red, the individual's full flight-or-fight adrenaline response has kicked in and all of the resultant generalized autonomic nervous system response mechanisms are energized and primed for action. Breathing becomes shallow and rapid, the heart beats with more power and frequency ("My chest was pounding!"), and blood flows from the digestive track and other nonessential functions to the muscles, which can produce tingling and twitching sensations and a feeling of queasiness. Note that people cannot endure this status indefinitely, and it may take a concerted effort to overcome the residual state of arousal after the threat has passed.

When traveling, being in Color White should only occur in exceptional circumstances. This level of relaxation might be appropriate when traveling in business or first class on a transatlantic flight and you happen to be the only passenger who is not a senior representative of a major religion traveling to an interfaith conference. In that scenario, you can likely afford to be oblivious and relax, daydream, nap, or otherwise enjoy blissful inattentiveness, surrounded by people of great spiritual accomplishment and integrity. Otherwise, since traveling and living abroad means being at a bit of a disadvantage, you should strive for a state of calm, relaxed, but nonetheless attentive vigilance: Color Yellow. When traveling into higher threat areas or situations, you need to raise your level of attention to Color Orange.

One of the best indicators for the need to shift up from one color to the next is the ability to perceive threat through surveillance detection. You can develop this competence by forcing yourself to pay attention to those little observations and trying to trace back those feelings of unease (e.g., *I'm being watched*) to the behavioral clues that led to those feelings.

Identifying Potential Threats

So, how do you know which stimuli in a new environment should be perceived as threats to either safety or security? What should you be on the "lookout" for? It is as useless to identify everything new in the environment as potentially harmful as it is to regard nothing as a threat. A risk management approach based on probability, opportunity, and intention makes the most sense. What is the probability that your safety or security will be imperiled by a particular aspect of the new culture? What opportunity do you present for those who would do you ill? And finally, what are the likely intentions of those around you?

Some of the sources of threat to safety include environmental and infrastructural elements over which you have no control. However, you can choose and use the most reliable hotels, airlines, buses, taxis, and other transportation services. These may cost more but they represent a statistically sound decision. On the security side, when an area of town is identified as dangerous, that means that the *probability* of falling victim to some untoward experience is higher. Wisdom dictates following the probability curve and staying away from those areas. Taking into account probability not only helps in reducing exposure but also helps you understand and realize that bad things do happen—sometimes with evil intent, and sometimes without—to good people, including you, and thereby serves to limit denial and delusions of invulnerability.

The second area to analyze in threat identification and perception is *opportunity*. In its largest sense, opportunity is that set of potentially fortuitous circumstances that allows an individual to experience some gain. We typically think of opportunity as a chance for *us* to benefit from some advantage. But there are others who want to experience gain, too, and who are driven to take advantage of any opportunity that you might present to them. Leaving your laptop in a carrying case on a hook or against the wall in an airport washroom while you tend to business is an example of providing an outstanding business opportunity to an airport thief. Walking out of a bar in a foreign city inebriated late at night after having paid your bar bill by fishing in your pockets for a fistful of local currency is another extraordinary business opportunity waiting to happen. Dealing with shady characters in back alleys to exchange currency at black market rates is another tremendous opportunity for someone else. Taking a cut-rate informal taxi outside your hotel may well turn into a marvelous chance for a local felon. There are nearly no limits to the opportunities that the traveler or expatriate might be able to provide to someone in the destination country—but Travel Wise sojourners can make smart decisions and choices to minimize those opportunities for others.

Of course there are people in your own country who are looking for those opportunities, too. How is this different? In your own country, you know the rules of the game and have developed locally appropriate street smarts—survival skills. Once abroad, the balance shifts to provide the home team the advantage—just as it does in the World Cup or the Olympics.

Finally, recognizing, analyzing, predicting, and judging the *intent* of others becomes a critical self-defense skill. This is made much more difficult by the lack of home-team advantage—by the differences in culture for the traveler to learn. For example, it is hard for many businesspeople to understand the extent to which criminals will go to wrest some competitive advantage. Bribing a hotel maid to have a look at a business traveler's room and copy the contents of a laptop hard drive onto a USB thumb drive takes seconds.

And in many cases, countries collude with private sector concerns in matters deemed to be of national competitive importance, and in a global economy that threshold gets lower and lower. The Internet service provider (ISP) the hotel makes available may well share information with host country intelligence services. Would people really do that? If the intent of a competitor is to compete, whether at the corporate or national level, the answer to the question is inevitably yes. Google's arrangement in China, in which the company was forced to compromise on its standards of protecting the free flow of information and the anonymity of users, is a testimony to the host government's willingness to do whatever it takes to serve its own interests.

Looking at safety and security through the lens of threat identification and perception, and understanding the interaction of probability, opportunity, and intent lets you predict and respond to threats to safety and security proactively, and thereby facilitate the management of risk.

Security Intelligence

In the same way that emotional intelligence focuses on self-awareness, self-management, social awareness, and relationship management, security intelligence starts with what you know about your strengths and limitations, expands with how well you are actually able to consistently use your skills and awareness, grows with understanding the variation of threat across cultures, and, ultimately, relies on your ability to develop and manage mutually supportive safety and security relationships in country.

In addition to the personal awareness issues raised in the inventory in Chapter 2, security self-knowledge includes the ability to tap into, trust, and use your sixth sense. In this regard, the sixth sense is perhaps nothing more than the subconscious part of the mind trying to add its voice, insight, and intuition to the day-to-day dealings of the dominant conscious mind. Perhaps this ability is the culmination of rapid processing of intuition and miniscule bits of observed but not recognized threat information. Wherever this ability comes from, being able to sense danger and calmly and efficiently react to it is part of the personal security awareness and management of a Travel Wise person.

Security intelligence also includes the ability to understand and deal with those around you. In this regard, social awareness in a security sense includes strategies for avoidance, mitigation, and resistance. By far, the preferred strategy for dealing with any threat is avoidance. Understanding and predicting threats, and planning to avoid those threats, is far easier and less costly than the alternatives. Another possible strategy is to plan for companionship—don't be caught alone. There is some safety in numbers.

There is also some safety in anonymity—finding ways to be inconspicuous despite being a foreigner, by modifying the clothing you choose to wear so that you don't sick out as much as you otherwise might, can help lessen your profile as a target. Another strategy that is particularly important for threats posed to security through crime and terrorism is to make a habit of being unpredictable. Simple behavioral changes, such as varying the time and duration of leaving your hotel room for breakfast, or varying your departure time and route as you drive between your residence and work, are very effective at proactively thwarting the malicious. Finally, managing your internal state as you interact with others by keeping Cooper's Colors in mind can help minimize your exposure to threats and maximize your ability to respond should someone decide to take the opportunity to try to snatch your purse or laptop.

Crisis Management

So what do you do when the fire alarms go off in a hotel, or the floor starts shaking violently, or you find yourself coming to consciousness on a curb with blood on your face and shirt from being knocked down and robbed by some goon on a motorcycle? Crisis management, of course, includes not only what you do during and in the immediate aftermath of a crisis but also what you do before a crisis hits to prepare, plan, and manage.

The first predictable element of any crisis, whether personal or a large-scale catastrophe, is that communication will suddenly become a huge issue. Even in countries with well-developed and advanced communications infrastructures, systems become overwhelmed when the number of people suddenly needing information spikes, like when Hurricane Katrina hit the U.S. and during the September 11, 2001 terrorist attacks: The number of desperate users suddenly exponentially surges and the telephone towers and equipment become jammed and/or go down. For the individual who has just had her vacation brought to an abrupt end by a thief or mugger, the need to communicate becomes enormous—with family members, banks and credit card companies, the police and the embassy, the airlines, and hotels for cancellations and changes in travel plans.

If communication is a predictable element of crisis management, what can be done in advance of, during, and after an emergency abroad to mitigate the problem? Building in redundant communications plans, as mentioned in Chapter 3, becomes critical.

The second predictable element of crisis management is that the emotions of those involved will suddenly become an issue. Anger, fear, confusion, and grief are difficult emotions to deal with in one's own home, and overseas self-management of these emotions becomes much more difficult and complex. A further complication is the difference in cultural norms, assumptions, and rituals around crisis management and dealing with the aftermath of tragedy or injury. Rape survivors, for example, may well be dealing with an unsympathetic bureaucracy at several levels, while they themselves are still in shock, hurt, and frightened. Dealing with stress becomes a critical self-management technique, and, in cases of severe injury or trauma, recognizing the possibility of ongoing psychological problems as a result of traumatic exposure becomes a necessity.

If international travel has exposed the traveler to gruesome or graphic experiences of death and suffering, and/or if the traveler herself felt that she was going to lose her life, or had a life threatening encounter, assault, or rape, the traveler may be returning home primed to undergo a very difficult readjustment process known as post-traumatic stress disorder (PTSD). The incident involving

St. Mary's College described in Chapter 10 is an example of the type of experience that may make travelers prone to PTSD, whether they were the students who survived the rape or were the colleagues who were forced to helplessly watch.

PTSD symptoms include difficulty sleeping, irritability, depression, exaggerated startle responses, hypervigilance, intrusive thoughts, dreams or nightmares of difficult experiences, and avoidance behaviors that seek to minimize contact with anyone or anything that might remind the traveler of the trauma he faced. By definition, these problems have to persist more than a month after traumatic exposure. The important thing to remember is that there are a number of effective treatments for PTSD— one needn't go on suffering. And the sooner treatment starts, the better the outcome is likely to be. The paradox is that for some individuals, the symptoms might not show up for months or even years after exposure to a traumatic experience.

Streets Smarts

Street smarts or savvy is simply a localized version of threat identification, perception, and effective response. It represents the ability to adapt and apply general security competence with new, location-specific information and achieve an integrated profile of behavior that reduces risk. This skill is what separates the internationally street-wise traveler from others and allows seemingly effortless adaptation in a variety of security environments. In essence, *international street smarts* involves taking generic and specific security skills and developing a personally appropriate solution that allows the traveler to achieve the purpose of his or her mission.

Personal Health and Medical Management

Because traveling and living overseas can often be stressful, the ability to maintain and safeguard your own health takes on larger significance than in normal life back home. In this context, the management of needed pharmaceuticals takes on new importance, as does attention to healthy eating, sleeping, and stress management. All of these factors are impacted by changes of location and culture. New health risks may challenge the traveler's immune system, and for some even adjusting to the slightly different chemistry of drinking water can cause debilitating digestive system problems. Figuring out how to resist the chocolates in Belgium, the beer in Germany, and the *masala dosas* in India can become a significant dietary challenge as well. Finally, should a medical emergency necessitate a trip to a local doctor or hospital, it is important for the patient to have faith and trust in the medical competence of those in country—or have an alternative planned in advance.

Fight or Flight—Getting Off the X

The last of the generic competency areas has to do with survival response. When all else fails and you are confronted with a life-threatening safety (e.g., an earthquake or hotel fire) or security (e.g., mugging, assault, or carjacking) situation, the ability to respond—to get off what security professionals call *the X*, can mean the difference between survival and disaster. Getting off the X can mean avoiding, escaping, or deciding to fight back with all of your ferocity, energy, and ability. (The X terminology comes from what is described as the kill zone in an ambush: getting off of it, getting away from it, or erasing it are the only options.) Some people have the ability to use that split second to quickly decide and act—fight or flight. Others freeze, become indecisive, or are too slow to grasp what is going on to react or escape.

Location- and Region-Specific Security Competency

In addition to the generic security competencies described earlier in this chapter, location- and region-specific security awareness and skills are vital safeguards for all travelers: from the short-term tourist through the long-term expatriate. There are two great sources for location-specific competence: experience and research. If you don't have experience, talking with others who have recently traveled to the country is a great source of information—but remember that the version of the threat that you will get from someone who has proudly and successfully negotiated the difficulties of adapting to a new security environment can be very skewed. Don't ask questions such as, "So, do you think it is safe to travel to [destination]?" Far better to ask questions such as, "What did you find you needed to do on a daily basis to safeguard your safety and security? What is the most probable danger that a newcomer will face?" Press colleagues to talk about the difficulties they faced at the *beginning* of their sojourns—*before* they had developed considerable coping mechanisms, including locally appropriate threat identification, perception skills, and street smarts.

Fortunately, for the intrepid who choose to venture where none of their friends or colleagues have, the Internet provides instant access to excellent travel advisories from ministries of foreign affairs of different nations. The U.S., British, and Canadian advisories[2] are all well written, frequently updated, and provide honest, if somewhat varying, perspectives on the advisability of travel. Each nation has its own political and organizational pressures to reconcile, as well as its bilateral relationship with the country for which it is providing travel advice: No country wants to be listed as a place that is too dangerous to travel to—the economics of travel are simply too important in a global age to write off. Nonetheless, if an advisory indicates that it is inadvisable to travel to a particular place, unless you are a mercenary or have some other totally compelling personal or professional reason for going, you are a fool to ignore the advice. As of this writing, all three consular warning systems advise against travel to any part of Somalia. That's

---

[2] I use these three countries because English is my native language and I am somewhat familiar with the three ministries involved in producing these advisories. Many other nations, of course, have web-based advisory systems of their own.

good advice. The British, of course, see no problem with going to at least parts of any other country in the world, including Iraq. The Canadians and U.S. Americans, evidently less bullet- and shrapnel-proof, strongly advise against travel there. So do I.

Given this global, free, high-quality information network, it is inexcusable to conduct travel or consider expatriating without studying the relevant threat advisories. In addition, the Appendix lists other resources. There simply is no excuse for not being current with the security situation in your destination country. These advisories are carefully written by experienced, sober, professional people. They aren't kidding.

CHAPTER 7

Making Sense of Your
Security Skills Profile

Having reviewed basic security skills, we will return to the Travel Wise Personal Inventory to see what your security profile says about you. We will also look at some logistical concerns and expand and deepen our examination of threats to your safety and security.

EXPERIENTIAL

Question 34: SELF-DEFENSE

Although it is unlikely that you will find yourself in a position in which it is advisable to use your martial arts skills in hand-to-hand combat in a foreign land, the confidence and fitness that attend serious martial arts training can provide a very strong security asset. On the other hand, the feeling of vulnerability that comes from feeling unable to protect oneself from physical assault makes adjustments in planning for travel all the more important. While any personal physical assault prevention training is valuable, overconfidence from taking a judo class 10 years ago can do more harm than good. In order for the training to have both actual protective value and to engender confidence, the training needs to be practiced and current.

Question 35: EXPERIENCE WITH CRIME/ASSAULT

Those who have survived crime directed against them tend to have a heightened sensitivity to and awareness of the threat of crime. Those who have survived several episodes of crime directed against them may either have a survival advantage in terms of their security through the resilience involved in having survived multiple instances of crime, or they may be more vulnerable through the trauma suffered in an earlier instance.

Confronting serious crime for the first time in one's life while abroad can seriously jeopardize an individual's ability to have a successful venture because of the direct physical or financial jeopardy, and the threat to one's safety—mental and physical—that may accompany the crime (an assault, for example). A negative experience can complicate or retard cross-cultural curiosity and learning and may erode motivation for accomplishing the original mission.

The painful questions those who have experienced and survived crimes against them need to ask is what would happen and how would they respond if they were victimized overseas. For those who have had the fortune not to have experienced crime against them, they should consider how an act of crime might influence their attitude toward the host country community and their missions. It is very hard for a person who has been traumatized by being the victim of a crime not to harbor feelings of hatred and fear toward the people of the host country, even though the crime was committed by an individual (or group) who hardly represents the culture at large.

Question 36: ATTITUDES ON SAFETY

If you checked the box indicating that you don't think about your safety on a daily basis, you are probably not entirely correct, but not at all in the minority. Each of us process hundreds of thoughts daily about our safety. We couldn't drive, walk across a street, step into a bath for a shower, or figure out what to eat without thinking about safety. If you live in an area with a particular geological or environmental threat, for example, an earthquake zone, tornado alley, hurricane coast, volcanic region, or drought or flood zone, you probably already have a great deal of survival information encoded in your brain about your safety from those threats. You might be quite right, however, in that you don't consciously think about your safety, nor go through a risk assessment and mitigation planning process on a daily basis. But that's a good habit to get into if you will be traveling.

As with tolerance for risk (Question 14), though, if personal safety is your daily priority to the extent that you plan your day around maximizing your safety, you are in for an unpleasant reality if you decide to travel. There is just too much that you cannot control—or even know about—when you travel abroad. What are the aircraft maintenance and repair regimens on the aircraft you will be flying? How well-tested and followed are the regulations for maximum capacity on the water taxis, boats, gondolas, ships, and other watercraft? How much does the host government pour into railroad track repair and upgrades every year? Who checked your hotel's compliance with the fire code, and when was that done? You will need to expose yourself to some safety risk because you cannot control all sources of threat to your safety.

Keeping your safety in mind as you plan your travels and each day's activities is just good sense. Do not rely on anything but the most reliable and reputable services you can afford for travel, food, and lodging. Think about contingencies—a "what if" assessment for each of the day's major activities. What if the cab ride back from Petra breaks down in the middle of the arid lands between there and Amman? Do you have enough water with you to comfortably survive a several-hour delay in the midday heat? Does someone know where you are going and when you intend to get back? Just a few moments of thinking through the challenges and the adventures of the day ahead of you can result in some lifesaving decisions.

Question 37: ATTITUDES ON SECURITY

Much of the same thinking for your safety applies for your security planning. Here you are concerned with hostile acts directed against you that are not necessarily personal—a pickpocket or mugger is unlikely to bear a personal grudge against you—but that target you with malicious intent. If you know from your reading that the train station in Cuzco, Peru is a thieves' den of pickpockets, prepare for your day by understanding that you will be exposed and vulnerable through the jostling, bustle, and crowds that you will endure at the train station. Don't take anything that you don't need. Do not plan your day so that you are coming home late and alone from a dinner in a strange part of the city. Put your valuables in a place that even the most talented of pickpockets—and some of them are really, really good—wouldn't be able to get to without you knowing it. A young third-culture kid who was traveling through Belize described how pleased he was that he got through an arts and crafts market in one of the roughest parts of town, known to be a virtual supermarket for thieves. He laughed as he told me that someone had lifted the equivalent of $3 in local currency from his pocket—he had no idea who or how or when it was done. He was very pleased that he came back with the $200 he had put in a plastic bag in his shoe.

The particularly pernicious thing about security awareness is that if you wait to start thinking about your security until you sense it is imperiled, it well might be too late. A few minutes spent considering the day's activities, options, and contingency plans can protect the investment of your travels and safeguard your mission. It can also help ensure that you don't have a spirit- and enthusiasm-deadening cross-cultural encounter of the worst kind.

Question 38: FIRE SAFETY

A friend who spent his career as a fire fighter, fire safety consultant, and trainer used to say that he knew two kinds of people in the world: Those who were capricious and unperturbed about fire safety, and those who had experienced a fire. He carried a small fire detector everywhere he traveled, and his travels took him almost every-where in the world. He would point out that this wasn't his own form of cultural arrogance—assuming that the countries into which he traveled had neither the infrastructure nor the code and regulations to ensure reasonable safety from fire. He took his little smoke detector and flashlight everywhere because he never knew who was in the hotel room next to his, and he had no idea what their practices were. Having seen first hand through a lifetime how quickly fire can travel, and how deadly its fumes can be long before the heat or sight of fire appears, he thought this habit was a reasonable and unobtrusive way for him to safeguard his life and the happiness of his family.

The central issue here is that assumptions about safety that are taken for granted in more developed nations, including arcane fire code regulations that few ever fully come into contact with in their own countries. There are fire code requirements for electrical service panels, wiring, switches, circuit breakers, insulation materials, framing, clothing, bedding and mattresses, kitchen ranges, hoods, alarms and detectors, water pressure, parking, stairways and elevators in buildings, escape windows, and countless other aspects of the physical environment. Since we rarely are required to deal with these wide-ranging regulations, it is easy to forget that, in combination, these fire code regulations make living much safer. And while traveling abroad, it is easy to believe that these protections are built in everywhere—why should you believe otherwise? The truth is far different. You should not assume that you are protected by rigid enforcement of comprehensive fire codes because, except for the most developed nations, it simply is not the case.

It perhaps sounds alarmist, since most people on earth have not experienced a life-threatening fire. But take it from those who have: You can never underestimate the great rapidity and finality of fire. If anticipating travel to an area in the developing world in particular, assume that fire-code protections that you may be used to do not exist. Faulty electrical wiring and breaker system overloads, the lack of fire alarms and fire-suppression technology in large buildings, and an inadequate firefighting capacity can all collude to spell disaster in even the most innocuous of situations. Fire kills mostly through toxic suffocation: Many victims of fire never realize that their last moments on earth are spent being poisoned by a fire that is taking place dozens of yards away.

Keeping in mind a few principles can go a long way toward mitigating this threat to safety. In general, accept a hotel room no higher than the fifth floor—in the event of fire, a hook-and-ladder fire truck won't be able to help occupants in a room higher than that. Carry a small smoke detector and a flashlight with you. Pay attention to the locations of fire alarm pull-stations, stairways, and other means of egress. Make a habit of counting the doors between your hotel room and the staircase (elevators do not function in fires). Keep a towel handy and if need be, wet it, wrap it over your face, and crawl as low to the ground as you can to escape. But most of all, keep fire safety somewhere in the forefront of your mind.

Question 39: ATTITUDE ABOUT POLICE

This survey question is designed to make you think about the unthinkable: What if you get to a country and find the police are untrustworthy? What if you find the police are less dangerous than the criminals themselves but perhaps also in league with them to some extent? How will your expectations about justice, safety, and security hold up in an environment where your basic assumptions about society are challenged?

The best attitude toward this question is that you neither trust nor distrust police. The most neutral, objective, and unbiased perspective will serve you best as you journey to other countries and interact with their infrastructures.

Question 40: WHERE WOULD YOU BE SAFER?

If you are contemplating a highly mobile lifestyle or extended multi-year stays overseas, you need to look at the big picture of your life and make sure you understand the long-term implications and significance of your decisions. There is no right answer here, obviously, only the one that most closely approximates your own reality, motivations, and desires.

If longevity is the goal of your life, the World Health Organization has some excellent maps on the best places to live for a long life. The fact that not many people want to live in those places should be irrelevant, since your goal is a long life. But looking into the quality of life afforded to a culture's senior-most citizens is research time well spent.

 **LOGISTICAL QUESTIONS**

Question 41: DO YOU HAVE MEDICAL INSURANCE?

This is one of the simplest questions in the survey to answer and analyze. If you are certain you are insured for any medical contingency during your travels, you are ready to travel. If you are not sure, or if you are not medically insured, you really need to stop and rethink your plans. It is hard to imagine the cost of an air-evacuation for a medical emergency that cannot be addressed in the country you are visiting. Without insurance, including air evacuation insurance, if you are traveling someplace where you would rather not undergo major surgery, you leave those who love and care about you with an impossible choice: Should they sell everything they own to pay for your medical evacuation flight in the hope that your life will be saved, or should they risk your fate to the facilities that are available in the country? This is very similar to the choice the loved ones of kidnap victims face. It is unfair for you to put them in this position. If you want to see the gorillas of Chad, that's your choice, but don't make it someone else's responsibility to rescue you when your appendix ruptures or you have a traumatic brain injury in a Land Rover collision.

Question 42: DOES YOUR MEDICAL INSURANCE COVER YOU EVERYPLACE?

One of the unfortunate surprises many rescue volunteers who went to assist those struck by the Boxing Day tsunami caused by the Indian Ocean earthquake in 2004 was discovering that their health insurance didn't cover them because they were voluntarily entering a disaster area. It's a pretty good bet that one's health will be challenged in a disaster area; lack of food, potable water, energy, sanitation, and communication systems failure all conspire to favor opportunistic pathogens including viruses, germs, vermin, and that strata of humankind who prey upon human misery.

For those adventurers who for whatever reason decide to go to active war zones, you are taking on enough risk as it is—having medical insurance that is void in war zones is an irrational dalliance with disaster.

Question 43: EMERGENCY MEDICAL EVACUATION COVERAGE

As mentioned earlier, medical evacuation (medevac) flights are extraordinarily expensive, and sometimes they aren't available at any price. A colleague who had medevac insurance and who was evacuated from the Democratic Republic of the Congo to the U.S. asked what the insurer paid to get him out on a chartered medical flight. The insurer was reluctant to give an exact figure but told him they had paid about $128,000 in U.S. dollars. Of course that was just for the medical evacuation flight. Other costs include follow up care in the evacuation location and the expenses related to shutting down the work or endeavor the traveler was engaged in. These costs become a very difficult reality for an uninsured individual, family, or organization to face when minutes might make the difference between death and survival.

Question 44: LIST OF POSSESSIONS IN STORAGE

For students or professionals on long-term expatriations, the storage of personal effects is part of the logistics puzzle that needs to be addressed. Cataloging your possessions is a time-consuming but necessary step in getting ready for your assignment. A quick way to do this is to go around your home or apartment and make a video of your belongings in each room. Duplicate the tape or disk and save a version on a hard drive for good measure. Property inventory programs are available to facilitate generating computer records of your things, but you may do just as well by creating your own spreadsheet. You should record a description of each item, including the brand name, model, serial number, the original purchase date, place, and price, and include an open field for any other remarks. This will greatly facilitate insurance claims in the event of loss, theft, or damage, but will also give your heirs a good idea of what you owned in case you don't come back. Send someone you trust a copy either electronically or on a disk or thumb drive.

IDENTIFYING SOURCES OF THREAT

So what other information should you consider in terms of your safety and security? Up to this point, the focus has been on your basic security and travel skills, attitudes, and personal experiences. But security competence also includes an awareness of the threats that you will confront that are external to you, those that are predictable almost anywhere you travel, and those that are specific to your destinations. The focus is on your ability to predict pieces of information which you will need, and your ability to track down and use it in lowering the risk you face wherever you go.

■ Health concerns: These include information on the incidence of major diseases, including Human Immunodeficiency Virus

(HIV) infection, Sudden Acute Respiratory Syndrome (SARs), Avian flu, cholera, yellow fever, Marburg virus, respiratory infections, intestinal tract parasites (such as amoebic dysentery, giardia, and worms), required immunizations, as well as verifying whether the country's medical infrastructure provides the quality of care that you will accept.

- Crime: The most probable personal security challenge travelers will face comes from crime. It is imperative that you research the scams, cons, tactics, and incidence of crime before you go. Rape, carjacking, and murder are life-changing or life-ending events. You absolutely need to understand the level of these threats before you travel. You need to appreciate the context of criminal activity: Have subpopulations in your target destinations reached the level of desperation or depravity that they will have no qualms about taking your life, or are they just after a carelessly unattended iPod, laptop, or purse?

- Infrastructure: The largest single cause of fatalities for U.S. citizens overseas is motor vehicle accidents. Every experienced traveler has stories of flying on an airline that had flight maintenance standards that seemed designed to wreak disaster on passengers. Motor vehicle traffic in some cities has gotten so bad that being a pedestrian seems to be an act of calculated suicide. Add to that food purity standards, building codes, and a global glut of unemployed urban youth with access to firearms, and even routine travel can start feeling like a real adventure in no time.

- Environment: There are some wonderful places in the world that suffer serious environmental degradation, which can become intolerable for travelers. Air and water pollution in Mexico City, Cairo, industrial cities in China, and in hundreds of other tourist and expat destinations throughout the world can be very challenging to adapt to. If you know you are particularly susceptible to these issues, talk this through with your physician and make sure you are as prepared as you can be.

- Corruption: Corruption is a culturally defined construct and changes its veneer to suit the needs of various pockets of society. Coming to an understanding of what the prevailing practice is, as a tourist, a vital part of effective travel. Do customs agents receive "tips" or a *dash*, or *bakshish*? For the businessperson, these concepts go to the central viability of the business mission. Not only do foreign business practices vary widely with what may be practiced in the home country; many countries impose stiff penalties on their expatriates if they are involved in practices that are defined in the home country as corrupt. For example, the Foreign Corrupt Practices Act bars U.S. businesspeople from engaging in conduct that, by U.S. cultural and legal standards, is considered corrupt. It doesn't matter that global competitors from other nations do not operate under the same restrictions, or that the host country's business culture has a completely different way of doing business. In these cases, careful attention must be paid to walking the line between two sets of business realities.

Espionage against Individuals

Most people in democracies feel little or no threat from foreign espionage. It sounds too much like James Bond—lots of fast, crazy people with guns and fancy gadgets. In reality, most espionage, whether conducted by government agencies or private services, is much more mundane. Going through the trash (dumpster diving) is a primary example. Listening in on telephone calls and tapping Internet e-mail sessions are much less glamorous, but are nonetheless routine parts of espionage conducted against private citizens.

Is there anything that you know, or anyone who you know, that would be of interest to a business competitor or to the host country's intelligence services? The reality here is that even if there is nothing about your presence in country that could possibly be of any use to anyone, there are people who do not know that. They may be operating under a different set of assumptions. If you have proprietary business information with you—in your mind or on your laptop—assume that you will be the target of espionage. If you work for a government or for a contractor that works for a government, assume that you will be the target of espionage. Assume that you will be monitored and act accordingly, even if you believe you're traveling to a "friendly" country. The primary responsibility of every nation's intelligence service is to protect—and thereby be friendly—to its own citizens without regard to its behavior toward others.

Civil Disorder

In many nations around the world, the struggle for political power is waged without regard to who might get wrapped up in its violence. Readers will remember that in 1994, Rwanda, a basically stable country, was turned into a genocidal bloodbath of outrageous proportions in the aftermath of the shooting down of the president's aircraft. In 2006, as Lebanon was in the process of slowly rebuilding and developing its business infrastructure, Israel launched an invasion that prompted massive evacuations from Beirut and caused enormous upheaval. Much less dramatic episodes of student or worker strikes, political party machinations, or security force overreactions can engulf and consume all who happen to be present at the time into a cesspool of violence. Staying away from gatherings, protests, and acts of civil disobedience will lower the chances of becoming involved in another nation's civil unrest.

Terrorism

Of life's great worries, statistically speaking, terrorism is almost nowhere. Although the press and media pound us all with lurid details of terrorism everywhere, the reality is that you are almost as likely to be struck by lightening as you are to fall victim to terrorism. The whole point of terrorism is to make an unrealistic threat seem larger than it is, but the reality is that you are far more susceptible to everyday, mundane threats to your safety and security than you are to terrorism. In the U.S., about 40,000 people die every year in fatal automobile accidents, and in the last decade about 16,000 people have been murdered each year. Terrorism, even at its worst moments, never even approaches the same order of magnitude.

Weapons of Mass Destruction (WMD)

Like terrorism, weapons of mass destruction can provoke immediate fear, and because the potential impact is so great for various forms of WMD, they provide instantly attractive grist for the news media, no matter how remote or unsubstantial the probability of the threat. The reality is that WMD, such as radiation, nuclear weapons, and chemical and biological weapons, are very high-maintenance, high-upfront cost, and high-skill weapons and that there are far easier methods of instilling fear and causing terror. A bomb made from fertilizer and diesel oil rigged with an ignition device to suddenly explode in an anonymous truck is a much more likely to be within the range of technical competence of those who choose to use weapons of indiscriminate destruction. The mass murderer Timothy McVeigh, who bombed the Alfred P. Murrah Federal Building in Oklahoma City, Oklahoma in 1995, for example, was operating at the upper limits of his technical competence. Had he tried for a more exotic method of terror and chosen a WMD—a "dirty bomb" or biological agent delivery system, for example—he may well have inadvertently killed himself long before he was able to senselessly murder others.

Nonetheless, the possibility exists that some terrorist state-sponsored group or extortionist might be able to mount a viable WMD attack. To understand the scope of these agents, we will take a brief look at the types of WMD and some of the strategies for mitigating the threat or limiting the scope of the damage. In many discussions of WMD, the amount of technical information offered soon becomes overwhelming, as most of us aren't particularly conversant in the names of esoteric toxins, bacterial and viral strains, radioisotopes, or nuclear throw weight. To further complicate the issue, discussions of WMD tend to be short on practical, behavioral advice, lack an overall context, and rarely deal with the most predictable element of human response—fear.

Fear is a normal response to threat, particularly a strange and unfamiliar one. There are a few things to remember that will help control fear. First, there are things that you can do to protect yourself—even if only marginally—in the event of exposure to a WMD event. Not everyone will die, and in fact the imagination and the media team up to have us believe the threat to be more dire and comprehensive that it ever, in actuality, could be. Furthermore, in the event of a WMD, one of the best things to do is to remain calm and rational. An individual who is overcome with fear and panic will help no one, particularly himself. The fight or flight response may well mimic some of the initial symptoms of an attack agent—including short, shallow breath, queasiness, and cold sweating—and mask symptoms that could provide clues to the nature of a toxic agent. Remaining calm also can be contagious in the same way that panic can be. There may well be in our futures a WMD attack of some kind, but that does not mean that everyone will perish or that the world will end.

If a WMD event is threatened or suspected, look for clues in the environment. If more than one individual—or animal—suddenly exhibits unusual behavior or symptoms, including pinpoint pupils, a sudden darkening of sight, shortness of breath, tightness, a running nose, drool, unusual odors, or if dead bodies are discovered with no signs of obvious trauma, a WMD assault may be occurring.

Radiation

The most likely weaponization scenario for radiation is the so-called *dirty bomb*. This is an arrangement of a conventional explosive charge mixed with or surrounded by radioactive material from any source that is scattered and widely disbursed by the explosion of the bomb. As with most WMD agents, lethality is a function of the ability of the agent to be concentrated in a small area. The very nature of the dispersion of the radioisotopes dissipates the concentration of radiation that they produce, and thereby lessens the potential lethality.

Beyond the destruction wrought by the conventional explosive device used to scatter the radioactive material, damage can result from either short-term exposure—primarily through inhalation—of short-lived radioisotopes, or from the much more persistent contamination of the area caused by longer-lived isotopes. It is unlikely that the dispersed radiation would cause radiation sickness or poisoning because of the low concentration. The primary source of danger, beyond the immediate conventional blast damage, would be an increased rate of cancer over a number of years for those who inhaled significant amounts of contaminated air.

Clearly this is an unwelcome scenario but hardly one that is worthy of pursuit for the terrorist: The most dangerous phases in terms of radiation occur as the terrorist assembles, concentrates, and mixes or surrounds the radioisotopes around the explosive! In any case, paying attention to the wind flow and escaping as rapidly as possible in a direction perpendicular to the flow of the smoke and airborne debris plume is the single most effective strategy for someone who survives the initial blast.

Nuclear Weapons

As with radiation, the use of nuclear weapons is quite complex and dangerous, and requires very sophisticated handling, assembly, and delivery systems. Assuming some one, group, or nation was able to buy a fully armed and triggerable nuclear device, there is still the problem of delivery. For maximum effect, the device would be triggered at some distance above the ground—dropped from some aircraft or delivered by a missile system. This tends to limit the possibilities for terrorists, who would need to either defeat or deceive the target nation's air security system.

The notion of a briefcase bomb, which captures the fearful imagination of the public, is possible, but also not probable nor particularly effective for mass destruction. In order to be moveable, the amount of nuclear material required would have to be sufficiently small that, along with the arming and triggering devices, it would be light enough to be carried as a briefcase—more likely a suitcase. Far more likely, a less compact and much heavier and more lethal device would be rigged into a shipping container or truck and detonated in the heart of the target zone. Most of the blast energy would be directed upward (or initially downward, and then redirected upward by the earth) from the point of explosion. All structures and buildings in the immediate vicinity would be destroyed, but they would also deflect and absorb some of the explosive shock wave, heat, and radiation energy. People within the immediate area would be instantly killed, but the area would be limited. Those who escape death from the initial blast would have to concern themselves with the nuclear radiation from the fallout and radio-contaminated debris. Again, moving perpendicularly from the direction of the prevailing wind would provide the most protection in the aftermath of a survived nuclear explosion.

Chemical and Biological Weapons

Biological and chemical agents both require very competent handling and preparation and must also be weaponeered in a way that delivers a sufficiently concentrated dose to a target. If the target is small—perhaps a building or tightly focused area—this becomes possible, but to deliver chemical or biological weapons across a whole city, for example, would be logistically problematic. Huge amounts of toxic material would have to be delivered to achieve mass casualties.

While the delivery challenges of both chemical and biological agents are quite profound, the danger is nonetheless real, and should some aerosol container or package be unleashed against a population, the only effective response would be to get away from the source of the release as quickly as possible. Unfortunately, because of the need to contain the danger zone, rescue personnel will require people who have been exposed to a contagious or transferable agent to be isolated until the toxic agent can be washed or neutralized. In practical terms, that means that if you suddenly find yourself surrounded by a number of people in puffy white or yellow containment suits with badly fitting head enclosures, you should do as they ask, remove your clothes, and submit to being washed or scrubbed with soap and water or other cleansing agents. This would not be a good time for modesty or anything less than full cooperation—seconds matter in exposure to toxic agents. And don't be afraid of antidotes—if an injectable serum is available, follow the directions, take a breath, and plunge it in. There may not be time for delay.

If you are outside the hot zone, escape as quickly as possible away from the source of the toxin, if it is known. If unknown, move perpendicularly to the wind.

For both chemical and biological agents, there are four mechanisms by which the toxin enters the body and becomes lethal.

- The first, and most vulnerable, is through inhaled air. Not only is the lung a remarkable evolutionary miracle for gas exchange, it is also a profoundly effective delivery system to the bloodstream. In the event of suspected exposure, everything possible should be done to protect the lungs. If nothing else, putting a wet towel, shirt, or cloth tightly in front of the nose and mouth can help filter out some particles—even filtering only 10 percent can provide a potentially lifesaving difference.

- The second route of entry is through the skin—the skin is porous and also breathes. Where the skin is particularly thin, the eyelids, for example, the body is especially vulnerable. That is why one of the first indications of toxic exposure is often beaded or dilated pupils—the toxin successfully crossed from the outside world to the inner eye. Washing off the agent as soon as possible is important, and seconds matter.

- The third route is through ingestion. The body really is a closed system with a protected, limited interface between the body and outside world, and the digestive system serves as a tube that runs through the body to allow contact with substances from the outer world—food and water—to be selectively absorbed into the body itself. Another marvel of evolutionary engineering, the digestive tract also allows access to the bloodstream for toxins that are ingested—either eaten or drunk. Here the mitigating strategy is complicated by the characteristics of the toxic agent. In general, trying to induce vomiting, if the agent is still in the stomach, is a reasonable step. However, there are toxins for which this is not a desirable course of action, but without a medical professional on hand and reliable information on the nature of the toxin, it is difficult to make the right choice.

- The final entry route is not one that is likely to be used in any mass weapon, for it involves injecting a substance through the skin directly into the tissues and/or bloodstream.

The reality of WMD is that the nuclear arsenals of the developed countries are in all likelihood the greatest source of WMD threat for humankind. Anything short of a global thermonuclear exchange will mean that some people will survive, particularly those who remain calm and take simple, rational steps in their own defense.

On-the-Ground Reality

The other part of safety and security threat assessment has to do with the opposite of threat—that is, it deals with the capacities of the various parts of the social protection network to shield you from harm in another country. Those protections, however, may be very different than those to which you are accustomed and therefore will present a safety and security challenge in and of themselves. Your pre-travel research should include finding reliable information on the following infrastructural elements of your destinations.

- Emergency response: One of the great comforts we have come to expect is a competent emergency fire, rescue, and medical infrastructure. Almost any child—even pets—have been trained to dial 911 in the U.S. in the event of a life-threatening emergency to activate a comprehensive and integrated response system that can take care of pretty much any emergency. But what happens when there is no 911? What if there isn't an available ambulance, or the fire chief demands payment upfront for his firefighters to battle your blaze? What if the fire truck is broken down, or the hospital is already filled past capacity?

- Police: Police departments and officers in every country share some elements of a common vocational identity that comes with wearing a badge. Beyond that, the variations in training, selection, leadership, discipline, and pay create enormous differences in the performances of police forces. Because police officers are given power beyond that of citizens, that power can be abused, and in situations of lax oversight, poor or nonexistent salaries, and/or hopeless challenges of understaffing, under-training, under-equipping, and political corruption, there is almost no hope that honest, trustworthy police services can be enjoyed by citizens and travelers alike. The most travelers can expect and insist upon is that their own embassy will be contacted and informed in the event of an arrest or other detention. Interactions with some police forces have been so problematic that even victims of serious crimes have suffered in silence rather than seek help from the police forces.

- Legal system: Law and the legal system under which a people live are central pieces of the collective cultural identity. Ideas of jurisprudence vary widely, and while all people share an inherent understanding of justice, what that justice means varies as widely as any other cultural element across the globe. Assumptions about crime and justice are deeply ingrained and rarely held up to the light of comparative scrutiny. To add to those vagaries, the reality is that justice is not objective, and those involved in the criminal court system are subject to the same weaknesses of abuse of power and greed that afflict all members of society. Expecting anything else is unrealistic. It behooves the traveler to understand the basic premises of the legal systems into which they are entering.

■ Political: One of the biggest blinders we suffer as members of a political culture is the tacit assumption that other nations' political systems, however they are called or subdivided, must be essentially like our own and therefore based on the same predictable assumptions about the respective rights of the people and the government. Nothing could be further from the truth. The tolerance of the government—or in some cases, of other nongovernmental but nonetheless powerful bodies—for the individual's span of civil rights and behavior varies greatly. Even when to outward appearances things seem to operate more or less as they do at home, there can be profound differences in political assumptions lurking beneath the surface. It is the job of the expatriate, even the tourist, to understand these differences and behave according to that awareness.

■ Hostile government: In cases where the host government is overtly hostile to the country from which you come, you can expect to be treated not as an individual with your own political ideology and sensibilities, but as a representative of an enemy government, whether or not you have anything to do with your own government. Any expectations you have that the host government will play by some set of universal rules of fair play are misguided.

■ Logistics: The last area to check out before your travel is the logistics of your travel and getting things done in your travel destination. The fact is that each country has its own bureaucracy, and as a traveler you are subject to that bureaucracy, with all its attendant strengths and weaknesses. Mail and telephone services, for example, may be considerably different from those with which you are comfortable. Strange fees and paperwork can pop up at almost any turn, in the most innocuous of daily activities. This is all simply part of the phenomena of crossing cultures. Watch others and learn from how they get their personal business accomplished. In any case, realize that the culture operates in the seemingly strange way it does not to torment you, but for you to learn as part of your entry rites of passage.

SECURITY COMPETENCE FOR WOMEN

Why should security competence be different for women than it is for men? There are many reasons why this is the case, and many avenues by which to pursue this conversation. In this book, we will focus on being effective overseas—on accomplishing the mission. To understand why security and safety are different for women, we will examine some predictable issues and use two examples of international travelers, both attractive American women who are driven professionals, one in the business realm and the other a development and nongovernmental organization (NGO) worker.

Dealing with Unwanted Attention

Going back to the Travel Wise survey in Chapter 2 and looking at yourself from the perspective of a host country national—a young or middle-aged male—might afford some insights. If you travel to a country where you look markedly different in skin color, stature, or eye and hair color, you are bound to attract stares that you might prefer to do without. To a male in your destination country, you will stand out. You may be one of just a few—or perhaps the only—woman who looks anything like the women that the global film and television industry uses as actresses. You certainly represent someone new, and therefore special, and perhaps even available. And if the life depicted in movies is accurate, all a young man has to do to find amazing, earth-shattering companionship is to attract your attention.

The various culturally specific methods of attracting the attention of women—with various degrees of tact or desperation—that men around the world use would serve as the grist for an anthropology text. From the coy to the vulgar, the desire of men to attract women causes all manner of unusual interpersonal behavior. Whistling, gesturing, facial expressions and contortions, grabbing, hooting, screaming, staring, stalking, obsessing, showering with gifts, and investigating are all within this behavioral realm. That this behavior can be the initiation of unwanted advances or even criminal assaults brings us back to the threat that might be posed to women travelers.

Here's the view of Angela, an American woman colleague who works for an NGO.

I have been thinking about all the strategies my friends and I used abroad to enhance our personal safety. First of all, I think that people—maybe women in general, or Midwesterners especially—have a tendency to be more friendly than necessary. I found it's okay to be courteous and nice, but I learned early on that my tendency to smile and make eye contact with the people I pass on the street caused me more hassle than I was comfortable with. It seemed that simply making eye contact with a male as I walk down the street is often perceived as an opening for unwanted conversation or verbal harassment.

To avoid unwanted conversation with a male passing along the street (which in many cases would result in unwanted touching or close-talking), I would not look him directly in the eyes, as often this was perceived as an invitation for conversation; nor would I look down. Instead I keep my head up and eyes looking straight ahead, but not at his face to avoid the eye contact. I felt that this showed that I was confident, that I knew where I was going and had a purpose or destination. I also generally tended to walk briskly for the same reasons.

Obviously sometimes there would still be comments or whistles or weird sucking sounds that would come even without the eye contact, but I found (after a long series of trial and error) that what worked best for me was to ignore it. This was one of the most difficult things for me to do since I felt that by not protesting the harassment that I was in essence condoning the behavior, but whenever I used a, let's say, more aggressive approach, it only seemed to encourage the behavior more and increase my own frustrations with the situation.

I don't pretend that I have found the secret to avoiding unwanted attention, but I think often the difficulty is being able to find some middle ground: there is a struggle to balance the desire to be open to cultures different than your own (which might be less progressive toward women's rights and equality) and to protect the values that make you American (a strong belief in women's rights, for example). I think it is helpful to know before going into a new culture what normal interactions between the local men and women are, and how a foreign woman might be treated differently by local males. I have in mind my stay in Macedonia where the town I lived in was primarily Muslim, and men and women didn't interact much at all with one another. So when a male would approach me with rude/sexual comments, I felt more confident in my immediate and aggressive blocking of these attempts since I knew his behavior wasn't even acceptable in his culture, let alone mine.

Not being too friendly was difficult for me and my friends. For example, if we did meet someone new and did have a pleasant conversation, it was hard to come up with a good excuse for why you will not give him your phone number— for which it seemed they invariably asked and were offended when you didn't want to give it to them. But experience showed that whenever a number was given out, there would be a ridiculous number of phone calls late at night and so forth. So it's hard, but I found it saves you a headache and sleep if you can find a way to politely avoid giving out your number. It seems obvious, I know, but within the context of the situation, it can be tricky to negotiate.

Other, general strategies were things like, when asking for directions (which I had to do a lot), I never gave the name of my hotel or where I was staying, and instead used a nearby landmark such as a church or shopping center so that whomever I was asking would not know where I was staying.

Mostly I think I tried to look confident, so as to not make myself a target any more than I already was, and to be nice but not too friendly.

Angela is a good example of having a combination of personal and interpersonal skills, emotional intelligence, security consciousness and awareness, cross-cultural insight, and is possessed of a driving sense of purpose and mission. It is clear from her narrative that she is very assertively responding to the security threat around her—she isn't hedging her chances on luck. She actively gathers and interprets information, develops strategies, tries them out, and refines them based on her experience.

And she clearly uses, and trusts, her intuition—her sixth sense. Following your intuition across cultures is a fairly messy business—you may well be wrong more often than you are right. But *if it feels wrong*, you should try to get in touch with those subtle signals that are making you feel a sense of unease—a glance, a gesture, a reflection, even a premonition. Try to identify what it was that triggered your gut instinct. Even if your intuition is nothing more than misguided interference of your subconscious self with your rational mind, in the event something did happen, your recovery could proceed unclouded by self-doubts over how you knew something was wrong and should have avoided some situation but pursued it anyway.

Deciding Who to Trust

Travel invariably exposes the traveler to new people. In every cultural context, there are those who are trustworthy and those who are not. Deciding who can be trusted becomes a critically important safety and security exercise for the wise traveler. Is this taxi safe? Does the driver have the skills to navigate the chaotic traffic? Is he a thief who will overcharge me, or is he a criminal who will set me up to be mugged? Is the hotel safe? Can you trust the lock box? The bellhop? The cleaning service? Is the hotel built to withstand a fire with a working, adequate sprinkler and alarm system? Can you trust the manager's assurances? Can you trust the employees by the reputation of the hotel chain?

Gauging the integrity and trustworthiness of people across cultural boundaries is a tricky business, but one that is essential to success in most overseas missions. Theresa, a business consultant who is constantly traveling the world to meet and work with a variety of clients, talks about her strategies for figuring out who she can trust.

> I watch people interact with one another. If I see certain behaviors in someone, I will not trust the person. If they are condescending or seem to come on to every woman in sight, I just won't trust them. I won't be open with them. I look for people who value their families, their significant others, their children, their home lives. If they talk about those people and things with respect and enthusiasm, that tells me that they are good people. I watch how they treat their subordinates. I watch to see if there is a difference in how they treat their peers and partners. I watch to see if they are duplicitous to others—as soon as they are, I won't trust the person because I know they won't have any qualms about lying to me either. I also pay attention to how self-centered and ego-driven they are. If they are always talking about themselves and their own accomplishments, and not sharing credit, that tells me the person is not trustworthy.
>
> I also look to see who has power in an organization, and I make a conscious effort to acknowledge that power, and build a relationship with that person whether I trust the

person or not. For those whom I do not trust, it is all about business, and I wouldn't think of including them in my private life.

I always prepare by trying very hard to understand the culture that I'm going into—to find something about it or within it to appreciate and to build common ground. I also try to engender trust by being more cautious, less optimistic than I normally am, because I know that many of my business partners dislike that element of Americans—I take it as a compliment when they tell me, "You are not like most (U.S.) Americans."

And I never mix business with pleasure. If someone asks me out to dinner after a business deal, I won't go unless there is a whole group of people going. If someone asks me out, I will say, "Hey, we should all go out" and actively invite others as a condition of going out at all. And if we all do go out, I will look for the senior-most guy in the group and ask, "Hey, can you help me get a cab so I can get back to my hotel safely?" I think they like that, they feel like they are in charge and take some responsibility for my safety. It builds trust by flattering their sense of importance and control.

I am conscious every day of being a woman, an outsider, and younger than most of the executives I deal with who are about 95 percent male and 98 percent older than me. I think about it every day as I get dressed—how I want to come across, how I can fit in. I am much more conservative in my business travels than I am in my own life. I have colleagues who use their sex appeal as part of their strategy. I consciously avoid doing that.

Outside of the business arena, I never trust people in positions of authority or power—customs officials or police— but I am respectful. You have to be respectful, and don't want to be perceived as flirting, but also need to build a relationship so that they will help you.

And when people get out of line, you absolutely have to be confident—not out of control—very firm to get people to leave you alone. But you really have to have that self-confidence. You cannot ever look like you don't know what you're doing or like someone can mess with you. You have to look like you are confident, that you know where you are and know where you are going.

And I almost never travel with a laptop. If I need to bring data, I will bring a laptop but keep the data only on a USB thumb drive that is encrypted. And I never leave that thumb drive anywhere—it is always with me. I just don't trust the safety of that data even in the best hotels. My Black-Berry [international cellphone and e-mail access device] is always with me. I can always call anyone, anywhere.

Theresa is a business-mission focused, cross-culturally competent, interpersonally effective traveler who understands the importance of safeguarding her safety and security, and makes it part of her daily practice to plan for it.

FINDING EFFECTIVE SUPPORT WITHIN HOST COMMUNITIES

In the book's Introduction, I described a threat to my safety and security as a Peace Corps volunteer in a little village in the Himalayas. One of the points of that story was to emphasize the importance of actively building networks of support within the communities and locations you will visit to use as local cultural informants—trustworthy host countrymen and women to provide reliable advice on safety and security issues. It may be with the hotel concierge, another student and her family, or the neighbors in your apartment complex. Reaching out and building friendships can provide an invaluable measure of protection for getting local, culturally accurate threat information and engender a sense of responsibility to help look after your security. For women, finding a host countrywoman of similar age and circumstance can provide vital clues on who, where, and what you should avoid to safeguard your security. Older people within the community can likewise provide vital information and link you into the more established part of the communities you visit. Befriending a grandmotherly or grandfatherly shop owner can create a powerful security resource.

THE IMPORTANCE OF YOUR SECURITY SKILLS

Security is a basic need for humans, and all of the open-mindedness, good intentions, intellectual curiosity, and preparation will be for naught if a traveler is the victim of a serious assault during his first night in country. Without security competence, the individual jeopardizes his or her mission. She will not develop the personal awareness, interpersonal interaction skills, or cross-cultural competencies and will struggle to maintain focus on her mission. As is the case on a national level, a society must ensure the safety and security of its people before they can develop socially, politically, economically, and culturally. So it is with the individual—without security, all energies are put into survival.

Developing your security competence therefore is a fundamental precursor to overseas effectiveness and success. Simply making a habit of paying active attention to your own security behavior and the threat environment around you can serve to greatly improve your chances for success in your international endeavors. And since your behavior and attention are under your control, there is nothing stopping you from developing this invaluable competence.

CHAPTER 8

Understanding Your
Motivations

It might seem that a careful review of the individual's or organization's motivation for traveling abroad is superfluous—something that is so obviously and routinely done that no further mention of it need be made. The truth is far different, however, and few international travelers really understand the full range of motivations that propel their behavior. Yet without fully understanding those forces, how can an informed decision of the value of a trip against its costs—both real and potential—be reached? How can an organization start the return on investment (ROI) calculations that allow business case analyses to take place?

In previous chapters you've seen examples of individual travelers and the challenges they faced. But in each case, there is an untold story of the dynamic flux of motivations that drive the behavior of the individual. The simple, honest answer to the question, "Why am I really going on this trip?" can be as elusive as it is valuable. Without that answer, simple choices can become complex and confused, and inappropriate conclusions and decisions reached.

Just as a business needs to conduct an assessment of return on investment before venturing into overseas markets, so must the individual. How much time, money, and energy should one invest in language and cross-cultural preparation? How well funded—both in terms of immediate money and reserves—does one need to be to ensure mission success? How much should normal activities be restricted because of an abnormal safety or security environment? How should one comport oneself? Is it appropriate to behave as a tourist? Or as an aspiring member of the new culture? Perhaps as a long-term partner?

Without understanding motivation, no rational assessment of risk is possible. Motivation is the clearest conduit to understanding the relative concept of travel value. Why is it worthwhile to face threats, and thereby take on risk, when that risk and those threats could be avoided merely by not going?

INVENTORY QUESTIONS

Question 45: WHAT DO YOU GAIN BY GOING OVERSEAS?

Think of this as the 30-second explanation to your grandmother about why are leaving. You should have a quick and ready answer, easy to understand, that truly resonates with your most deeply felt motivations. Practice saying it to yourself. When your business travel takes you all over the world and barely leaves you time to get your laundry done in between trips, and friends and family assault you with "Why do you have to travel so much?" you should have an answer ready that gives them that instant of insight that will get them to relax. "I love my work—I can't even begin to explain how much I've learned in these travels . . . ." "I'm trying to get in as much travel as I can now to position myself for a promotion that I really want . . . ." "It is exhausting, but I feel like I only get things done when I'm on the road—I just get frustrated by staying in the office . . . ."

Whatever the reason is, you should have a public relations version of it ready for dissemination. Sometimes a carefully thought-through sentence or two can both ease nervous—and perhaps frustrated—family and friends, and remind you of why it is you are doing what you are doing.

Question 46: WHY ARE YOU GOING?

Your motivation is at the core of predicting your mission's success in traveling. Are you going on a business trip to make a sale, or are you going so that you can make some sales to demonstrate your business acumen and support your career aspirations? Are you getting away from a bad relationship or are you trying to revitalize your own life? Are you going because you must—it is your duty— or are you going because of who you are and because of your awareness that you need to remain true to your identity and to whom you aspire to be? Is that exchange program a way to get away from campus and get some easy credits or is it a brave exper- iment to expose yourself to a new world?

The decision to go to a war zone, except for those who are compelled by military service requirements, is one that should be taken with grave responsibility. There are a number of people for whom this kind of scenario is seen as an opportunity: international journalists, stringers, and camera and video reporters; humanitar- ian assistance workers; doctors; mercenaries; and people who are drawn to the sometimes lucrative hazard pay schemes to provide otherwise mundane services, such as truck drivers and engineers. Whatever the reason, the first step the traveler needs to take is to get clear on what his or her own motivation is and weigh that against the hardship and risk.

Once that decision has been reached and communicated within the individual's own support network, the traveler needs to care fully think through the full gamut of contingency planning scenar- ios that may be possible—starting with the Travel Wise Personal Inventory. It is important to talk firsthand with someone who is currently or has recently returned from the same theater of op- erations. The prospective traveler should try to find someone as close as possible to where he will be going and who is in a similar situation in life (married or single, male or female, 20-something or 60-something, etc.) to discuss a full range of candid survival issues.

MOTIVATION JOURNAL QUESTIONS

Take some time to consider the following questions. You can use these questions as a basis for a "motivation journal" to analyze your reasons for wanting to travel.

- Do you need to go? Why?
- Do you want to go? Why or why not?
- What will happen if you don't go?
- Is there someone else who should go instead of you?
- Is there a better time for you to go?
- Would delaying the trip sacrifice its overall value?
- Is the trip worth the expense in time, money, and effort?
- Is this trip worth dying for?

Honest answers to these simple questions will yield a gold mine of information that can help you be a more secure, informed, effective traveler. There are no "right" answers, but the best answers are those that come closest to the truth of your reality.

Is it worth it to risk your job and pay exorbitant last-minute international flight charges to travel to a conflict-torn area to see someone you just met last week? It might be if you are in love, for example, and think you've found *the* person—the life partner—you've been dreaming about. Even if the romance doesn't work out, the lesson learned might be worth the cost of the trip. No one but you can put a value on your desires. A civilian colleague told me that he thought his third trip for a year-long deployment to Iraq was worth it to him—he certainly didn't have to go—because the work he was going to do was what he had been training for all his life and was the epitome of the identity he held of himself. Not going would mean sacrificing who he wanted to be—a profound existential threat to a deeply authentic person and committed professional. I asked him if it was worth his life. He said, "I don't look at it that way. I understand that I might be killed—the threat is real and I know it—but I also understand more clearly than ever that this is my life. This is what it is about." This is the same answer that I would imagine Fern Holland, the former Peace Corps volunteer and women's rights lawyer, and U.N. envoy Sergio Vieira de Mello, both of whom were killed in Iraq, might have understood and shared.

So what is motivation as it applies to travel? Is it about self-actualization and fulfillment? Of course, it can be driven by the need for affiliation, inclusion, and sense of belonging. Most refugees travel because of more basic survival needs—food, water, the hope of safety from natural or man-made catastrophes ranging from earthquakes to genocide. The value of travel to someone escaping civil chaos, war, genocide, or drought clearly has a different meaning, intensity, and imperative than it does for the exchange student who longs for adventure spending time on an Israeli kibbutz. In the former case, travel represents the only hope for survival, fraught as it may be with immediate inherent dangers. In the latter, there is increased exposure to threat as a result of travel, and the calculation of risk must include both an assessment of the actual danger as well as the value of the trip to the traveler.

MOTIVATION INFLUENCES BEHAVIOR

Beyond providing fundamental risk assessment information, a clear-eyed analysis of the motivation for travel is important because motivation influences behavior in ways both profound and quite subtle.

Although the pioneering work of humanist psychologist Abraham Maslow's on the Hierarchy of Needs has been challenged and refined by various authors, scholars, and researchers, a basic version of the model offers both wide familiarity and a handy tool to explore the notion of motivation and travel. The elongated triangle behind the Travel Wise Model represents Maslow's Hierarchy of Needs. That it underlies the competencies—personal and interpersonal awareness, cross-cultural sensitivities, and security skills—is no accident. Motivation and need form the bedrock of understanding the model. Let's briefly review Maslow's model to help reacquaint ourselves and tie in motivation to travel.

At the very bottom of the graphic pyramid of Maslow's model, the basic physiological necessities of human beings, including food, water, sleep, and shelter, form the base upon which other needs develop. Without satiating—or at least finding some minimal accommodation to these needs, the individual cannot focus on meeting higher lever needs. This becomes obvious, for example, in the behavior of food, water, or sleep deprived individuals. Moving up the pyramid, the next set of needs center around safety and security needs, including economic security (freedom from poverty). Next comes social needs—the need to *belong* and to feel part of a society. Completing the lower four deficiency levels of the pyramid (so named because the deficiency of any level precludes movement to the uppermost level) humans need to feel esteem— that is, their egos compel them to need to feel rewarded, valued, and to appreciate that their existence matters. When these four levels of needs are met, some individuals continue to seek growth and find actualization in the uppermost cap of the pyramid. Research and other theories that have evolved since Maslow's hierarchy demonstrate a somewhat more complex and nuanced reality behind human motivation.

Regardless of the shortcomings of the model, Maslow gives us a point of departure for beginning to understand what drives people to leave the comforts and predictability of home to travel abroad. The wide range of motivations for travel all fall into one category or another: financial gain, career promotion, education, horizon expanding, visiting and reconnecting with friends and relatives, relaxation, escape, change, or an inner drive or calling that cannot be satiated without traveling. All of these motivations are of course prima facie rationales for going abroad. The point of understanding motivation is not to categorize types of motivations, but to reach a point of clarity about which needs and desires are being met, so that some rational value may be attributed.

LeAnne, a university colleague, works for a multinational image-consulting and advertising firm. She has been working with a client in Madrid that has necessitated a half-dozen trips in the last three months. The group representing the client wants her to go again, although they admit that they can get the same work done through a videoconference. Theresa is ambivalent about the trip; she's tired of the traveling and suitcase living, but she likes working with the client and thinks that although the work could be accomplished in the videoconference, there is some element of her personally going there that seems somehow more loyal to the client. To complicate things, she is working with several other clients who are getting ready for an election cycle—the busiest and most lucrative time for image consultants. She also has been dealing with a needy friend who is going through a divorce, and there is an outside chance that her current romantic interest, a military officer assigned overseas, may be coming back to town for a conference.

She ponders what she should do. They don't really need her to go, she thinks, and she really would like to be at home for a number of reasons. So why should she go? What can she get out of the trip that would make the travel worthwhile for her and for the client? She goes through the questions listed earlier for the motivation journal. Does she need to go? No, not really. Does she want to go? Maybe—she wants to be responsive and loyal to a favorite and highly valued client. What happens if she doesn't go? They will do a videoconference and everything will probably be okay. Is she the right person to go? She's the only person who can go. Is there a better time to go? Would delaying the trip help? No, one way or another, the client needs the support now, not in several weeks. It's either the travel or the videoconference, but in either case it has to be soon. Is the trip worth the time, money, and effort? That's the big question. Is it worth dying for? No, of course not, but the likelihood of dying in Madrid, despite the train station terrorist attacks of 2004, is nearly nil. Weight gain from eating phenomenal tapas and drinking Rioja is a more likely threat.

In the end, after thinking about her answers, she realizes that she needs to go not because the travel is the only way to get the work done, but because she and her clients share an affiliation that goes beyond a business transaction. They have been good to her and she feels loyalty to them. In the end, her values around protecting a hard won and carefully maintained set of interpersonal relationships with a key client make the trip worth the expense of going. She is not overjoyed about reaching that decision, but now, at least, she fully understands why she has to go.

Earlier in this book, the case of a high school student desperately seeking adventure by going to an Israeli kibbutz is mentioned. *I just want to go!* is an understandable but hard to quantify or rationalize justification. Perhaps one or more of these possible motivations rings particularly true for the young fellow: the possibility of an amazing cross-cultural and personal adventure, a sense of self-confidence, independence, world citizenship, or personal development and growth. What if we asked him to prioritize which of these motivations is most important to him? Perhaps he'd come up with a list like this:

1. Independence
2. A sense of self-confidence
3. Personal development and growth
4. The possibility of an amazing cross-cultural and personal adventure
5. World citizenship

The top three goals he lists can be achieved anywhere in the world, including where he lives now. In fact, the travel might jeopardize those top three. After all, can independence be bought by spending Mom and Dad's money to go work in a collectivist enclave? This prioritization might suggest that those three issues get resolved first, before the travel begins, as part of the lad's emotional intelligence and personal awareness preparation. The following alternative prioritization might suggest a different level of preparedness:

1. The possibility of an amazing cross-cultural and personal adventure
2. World citizenship
3. Personal development and growth
4. A sense of self-confidence
5. Independence

This prioritization reflects the self-actualization tip of the motivation hierarchy and suggests that the more basic needs of the young man have already been resolved. The value to a young man of the opportunity to have a self-actualizing experience can make the same financial investment seem like a bargain.

The important part of working toward clarifying motivation is that when a realistic assessment of the value of travel is reached, a rational assessment of risk can be started.

MOTIVATION'S IMPACT ON THE OTHER COMPETENCIES

Clarity around motivation makes rational risk assessment possible, and therefore is a fundamental part of safety and security competence. Without understanding the motivation, and hence the value of the travel, it is impossible to answer the very simplest of questions: *Is it worth the risk to go?* That the value of the trip cannot always be quantified is part of the complex reality of our lives. The motivation, the value of the trip abroad, should be clear and specific enough to allow the traveler to rationally weigh the value against the possible threats and thereby manage the risk on an ongoing basis.

Imagine how much more cross-culturally resilient a traveler becomes when she is empowered with a clear and driving sense of mission. The inevitable slights, moments of awkwardness, confusion, discomfort, and embarrassment become minor irritations against the backdrop of a clear goal. "I'll simply try again" becomes the prevalent strategy instead of suffering a sense of defeat. Cross-cultural resilience is a side benefit of clear motivation. Similarly, as was shown in Angela's and Theresa's narratives, a clear sense of the end goal predisposes the traveler to be more flexible, innovative, and persistent in awkward or difficult interpersonal dealings. It enables travelers to find the energy to "play the game" in a foreign culture that is required to get the job done. Motivation is almost a magical catalyst in creating success in international business and adventure.

Clarity around motivation applies to the NGO circuit rider contemplating an assignment in Dafur, Sudan, and to the vacationer wondering whether it is safe to go to the Caribbean during hurricane season. It applies to the person thinking about a cruise to get away from a failed relationship and a bitter, acrimonious separation. And, as will be seen in the next chapter, the same rationale applies to organizational risk management.

CHAPTER 9

Organizational Security

This chapter covers a broad overview of organizational security and includes a discussion of prudent risk management principles and strategies. This discussion will benefit those whose areas of expertise and responsibility typically fall outside the realm of the security professional: corporate officials involved in any aspect of international business, student exchange program administrators, NGO country project and contract managers and staff, and government officials at all levels of national, state, and local government who have international business dealings.

Organizational security, in essence, is the sum of the organization's personal security awareness, competence, and practice. Locks, closed-circuit TV (CCTV), rigorous safeguards, solid policy and planning, and top-level support all are important parts of the organizational security puzzle, but when it comes to getting a mission accomplished safely, it all depends on the aggregate of the security competencies of individual employees. It is in this regard that the Travel Wise Model comes back into play: The security competencies of those individuals are enhanced by their personal and interpersonal skills, emotional intelligence, cross-cultural competence, and the clarity and alignment with which they attempt to accomplish the organization's overall mission. When the individual's goals and motivation are aligned and in harmony with the sponsoring organization's mission, the result is greater organizational security.

If your organization is large enough to employ a professional security staff, count yourself among the lucky. Nothing can replace the diligence and vigilance of an organizational officer whose every waking hour is spent thinking about mission security. For most organizations, though, security is an added on responsibility for someone whose main job is accomplishing some specific part of the organization's mission overseas. In the former case, negotiating the safety and security policies against individual instances of exceptions and the need for flexibility with the security office will be an ongoing—but healthy and important—tension. This tension arises naturally as the behaviors and practices which safeguard an organization from threats to safety and security might interfere with the organization's mission success, thereby necessitating individual, case-by-case exceptions to security policy. It is in this regard, as you will seen later in this chapter, that common, collective clarity on the overall mission becomes critical. But there will be times and instances in which the organization's security dictates will seem overly restrictive, and the organization's own security personnel may seem to be if not the enemy, at least fully engaged in working against progress toward accomplishing the mission. This is simply the nature of international security. Businesspeople want to get out there and take risks and make things happen, but security people don't want bad things to happen, some of which are inevitable when taking risks. It can become as tricky as negotiating another culture, and in a sense, it is exactly that. The underlying values and assumptions of both groups are different, as are their strategies and thought processes. Some conflict and disorientation is inevitable.

If you have inherited security as an ancillary responsibility along with your main job, you will need to spend time and energy learning about the threats and resources that will weigh into your specific risk analysis. Any organizational mission can be imperiled by inattention to safety and security issues. These threats and resources must now become your issues. The lesson you can glean by reading about the St. Mary's College study tour in Chapter 10 is that your subject matter brilliance and expertise can be rendered an organizational liability by being inattentive to security.

UNDERSTANDING THE ORGANIZATION'S MISSION

In Chapter 8 you saw the power and importance of motivation for the success of the individual traveler and expatriate. For an organization, the mission is the very lifeblood of the international program. Whether the mission is to make money, establish a beachhead, expand the market, contribute to another nation's development or infrastructure, education and cultural exchange, or to develop group tourism, the mission is what makes the investment, and the risk, worthwhile. Just as it's important for an individual to understand his motivation, a lack of clarity around the mission can itself become a threat to the success of an organization's international effort. Only by fully understanding the mission can the personnel involved in an organization's efforts abroad make intelligent decisions about risk management for the threats that will be encountered.

VIEWING THE MISSION FROM THE STAKEHOLDERS' PERSPECTIVES

One way to gain clarity of the mission and its value is to look at it from a variety of points of view that go beyond those of the organization's operational leadership. Essentially, who cares if the mission is—or is not—accomplished? Obviously, the matrix of stakeholders will differ for each organization and situation, but getting in the habit of finding out who cares about the venture, and analyzing how much they care, directly informs calculations of the mission's value. For a student exchange program, the obvious stakeholders are the students themselves, their parents, friends, and family members, as well as those who are concerned with student affairs and the overall reputation of the university sponsoring the program. Other stakeholders include the students and faculty of the hosting university, and those involved in housing and caring for the students.

How much do they care? Imagine how the host families and classmates of the Syracuse University students who died aboard Pan Am 103 cared about them. Imagine how the parents cared, the university, its provost and president, and the dean and faculties of the schools from which the students came. If this seems too dire an analytical approach, remember that if a tragedy strikes a program, the parents, the classmates of the students, and the school officials will want answers about why it happened and will assume that it shouldn't have happened. In the absence of compelling evidence to the contrary, they will be inclined to blame whoever is running the program, whether or not that assessment is based on any rational appraisal. The power of the emotions at the time will push people to decide with their hearts—not with their minds.

Similarly, as we see with the many multinational contractors who have personnel in Iraq, when there is a loss of some sort, through kidnapping, assassination, bombing, or the inadvertent mishaps of doing business in a war zone, the family members of the deceased will blame the parent company for not taking better care of its employees. The statement that, "All of our employees were aware of the peril that they faced and were being well paid to face those risks" may sound reasonable in the public affairs office of the parent company, but it will do little, if anything, to assuage the anger and animosity of the survivors, and may well stoke their fury. As has been the case in Iraq, contractors who issue such statements also tend to sabotage the morale of the remaining organizational personnel, who will inevitably come to feel that (1) the company doesn't care about them, and (2) they are foolish for accepting whatever amount of money for what looks essentially like a cold financial transaction with their lives.

Other stakeholders, of course, include the company's stockholders, who are expecting that the overseas venture will be profitable, the more so, the better. If Burger King decides to sponsor a franchise in Beirut only to see the front windows shot out and pipe bombs scare customers away, the stockholders will fear not only for their equity in the particular franchise, which may well be negligible, but will fear the perception of damage to the corporate image and name. Stockholders of pharmaceutical companies will be reading the papers and talking to their market analysts about the possibility of a stock price nose dive based on the outcome of clinical trials, regulatory decisions, and litigation based on the impact of the product on the market and the patients.

Customers are another key stakeholder group. When the press reported that small toys sold by Mattel through the Toys "R" Us chain were potentially toxic due to the lead in the paint used to color the toys, the repercussions caused shockwaves among anxious parents who had grown to associate those brands with safe higher-quality merchandise. These companies didn't reach out to global manufacturers to sabotage their companies' most valuable assets—their reputations. But by outsourcing and exercising lax control over international suppliers, those companies endangered their status.

ASSETS AND RESOURCES

An organization's property comprises a range of both physical and nonphysical items. The following sections consider these assets and resources:

- Intellectual property
- Planning
- Knowledge and information
- Crisis management plans, rehearsals, and protocols
- Communication management

Intellectual Property

We are clearly in a post-industrial age in which ideas are the new currency of manufacture and trade. Whether those ideas come in the form of products, processes, or personal services, they are part of a company's net worth and can be described collectively as intellectual property. If intellectual property is a company's most valuable asset, it follows that it must also be the most significant source of vulnerability. Protecting this asset becomes a matter of survival, for without the ability to safeguard intellectual property, that property loses value and reduces the organization's net worth.

Planning

It may seem a strange and quintessentially nonliquid asset, but careful planning is important not just for achieving an organization's goals, but also for safeguarding intellectual property, contingency planning, business continuity, and crisis recovery. These all provide value by shoring up the organization against catastrophic loss. Unfortunately, this sometimes doesn't become obvious until there's a security breech.

A distinction can be made between *proactive* organizational efforts to manage threat and *reactive* responses. A robust proactive response includes corporate policies, workforce training, crisis planning, crisis management exercises, active intelligence and information gathering, situation monitoring, ongoing relationship building within the host country community and power structures, and top-level attention to the threat environment. Reactive response measures include emergency evacuation, crisis communication, and implementation of the business continuity plan. All of these measures, both proactive and reactive, are predicated upon a permissive operating environment; that is, a situation where there is some infrastructure, rule of law, functioning political and judicial structures, and where hostility is not at the level of direct and immediate threat to the lives of the workforce. In a nonpermissive environment, all bets are off, and the value of the mission has to be critically evaluated against the potential loss of life and property.

Knowledge and Information

The value of knowledge and information is becoming ever more apparent as global networks of hackers and malicious cyber freaks demonstrate an ability to disrupt normal operations, integrity, and the trust, confidentiality, and security of corporations by gaining access to the organization's information. Data is exchanged between laptops, desktop computers, and servers within a company: prices, customer lists, inventories, schedules, targets, records, communications, policies, and financial transactions all are part of the informational blood flow of an organization. That flow is a massive asset that must be carefully protected. A stolen laptop that compromises the records of employees and clients is an enormous threat to any organization, and particularly so when abroad, where the support infrastructure to do remedial damage control and correction may not be readily available—or cooperative.

The first step in protecting an organization is to raise the awareness and investment of each employee, foreign or domestic, in the critical value of data system integrity. One compromise can mean catastrophic loss not just for the organization, but for the individuals associated with the organization as well, as anyone who has suffered identity theft can attest. No one likes dealing with computer security systems and or memorizing different, complex user ID and password combinations. But short of an absolutely reliable biometric or other technical positive identification measure, passwords are all that keep our identities, and the invaluable information of our organizations, from the hands of global criminals.

Crisis Management Plans, Rehearsals, and Protocols

The difference between an organization that plans and rehearses for problems and one that doesn't becomes all too clear in the aftermath of any crisis. Crisis planning and rehearsal helps not just because the training helps individuals know how they should behave and what they should do, but also because the very process of understanding that something can—and may well—go terribly wrong gets people psychologically prepared to deal with the shock of the event itself. This kind of preparation actually has an immunizing affect against panic.

At a minimum, a crisis management plan should include action to accomplish the following:

- Delineate roles, responsibilities, and alternates (in case the primary person assigned responsibility for a particular set of tasks is unavailable)
- Identify fiscal, material, and mobility resources
- Control communications flow and media coverage
- Articulate loss and death notification responsibilities
- Detail the alternate command center as part of a business continuity plan
- Describe some trip wires—criteria identified in advance by which critical decisions can be quickly made

As with any plan, if those who are supposed to implement it are unaware of its existence, or haven't practiced and rehearsed its implementation, it is probably better to have no plan at all and rely on the recovery instincts of the workforce and its leaders. Trying to pore through a crisis management manual when people might be frightened, disorganized, not thinking clearly, and on the verge of panic is just courting disaster.

COMMUNICATION MANAGEMENT

Communication management is another asset available to the Travel Wise organization. Often the first response of officials in the aftermath of a crisis or disaster is to try to deny or cover up the extent of the problem. This is exactly the wrong approach. The disaster will attract media attention, and no matter how meddling and nettlesome this attention may seem at the time, it is a gift. Use it as a global microphone to tell your side of the story. As long as the organization indicates that it understands something is wrong and that it is a serious problem, that the company is doing everything it can to find out about the problem and remedy it, and that the company will be an honest and conscientious partner in sharing information as it becomes available with the media, the company has every chance of using the media to its considerable advantage to recover gracefully from the situation.

It is when company officials seek to avoid, deny, downplay, or lie about the scope of the problem that the company loses its value in the eyes of all of its stakeholders. Someone has to be tasked with addressing all of the various stakeholders and their concerns. Information needs to fly out to satisfy people's insatiable need for updates and reassurance in the aftermath of a crisis: to the home office, the employees and their family members, the neighboring community and business partners, the host government at all levels, and anyone else who will listen. The highest ranking official available should be briefed and put in front of the cameras to express the company's total commitment to make things right, express sorrow at damage or loss caused, and demonstrate integrity and honesty in the face of embarrassing information. Often a company's legal advisors will advocate against this course of action. But they are wrong; the truth will come out anyway, and then the company will wind up being more exposed to liability because of efforts to cover up the situation. Furthermore, and most compellingly, the company will almost surely fail at its original international mission by alienating all of its stakeholders—the community, the government, business partners, and consumers—who want to believe in the reputation of the company.

Here is where the emotional intelligence of the company's leadership becomes a make-or-break factor in mission success. Leaders who understand that crises are by definition emotional upsets that require open and honest leadership will find a way to be courageous and authentic in demonstrating care and concern for their employees and the surrounding community. Leaders who try to "manage" the crisis by ever more frantic attempts at rationalization, excuse making, and hiding behind the scenes in frenetic activity in their command centers will fail.

Author Gene Klann in *Crisis Leadership*, a publication of the Center for Creative Leadership, describes leaders who try to bully and intimidate others during times of crisis as being innate failures. Demonstrating a caring, concerned attitude engenders trust and loyalty. Ambassador Prudence Bushnell, the leader of the U.S. embassy in Nairobi, Kenya when it was bombed in 1998 by al-Qaeda operatives, became a legend in the U.S. foreign affairs community by demonstrating just that sort of leadership. Kenyan and American employees alike—and their family members—knew that she cared personally about each and every one of them and grieved the loss of so many colleagues and completely innocent Kenyan citizens. To this day, those who survived the bombing look to her for continuing leadership and support in almost a spiritual way. She was honest and deeply committed to making things right in an impossible situation, and she demonstrated heart, courage, and integrity. The embassy found a way to open for business the next day. The terror that al-Qaeda hoped to generate by killing unarmed diplomats and Kenyan citizens (most of the victims were young Muslim women attending a secretarial college next door to the embassy) backfired. The Kenyan–U.S. bilateral relationship actually strengthened.

Whether you are charged with the exchange experience of five college students from your university or the operation of a major international division of your corporation or a Royal Navy Marine brigade, understanding the strengths and resources that you bring to the table allows a rational definition of mission to be articulated. That mission, clearly understood, becomes the basis for risk analysis and management and empowers strategies for minimizing the threats you face.

RISK MANAGEMENT

After coming to an understanding of the value of the organization's mission abroad, the next step is to define the threat. A *threat* is any force or action that endangers the organization's mission or its employees. The threat can be further defined in terms of the *probability of occurrence* and the *impact* on the organization's mission if a threat occurs. It is in fully understanding the value of the mission and the nature and consequences of the threat that risk can rationally be assessed and wise decisions made. The following sections discuss those threats—terrorism, kidnapping, industrial espionage, and embezzlement and other employee crimes—and what you can do to minimize exposure to them.

Terrorism

The risk of terrorism to corporations and organizations is only slightly higher than the risk to the individual. Corporations that are clearly identified with a parent country, regardless of the multinational nature of their business, may become targets through the symbols that they offer the terrorist. Still, the terrorist threat itself is reasonably low. In the U.S. State Department's April 2007 publication *Country Reports on Terrorism*, in 2006 there were 28 private U.S. citizens killed as the result of terrorism. Lightning killed almost twice that number of U.S. citizens in the same time period.

Kidnapping

It is an irony of civilization that this barbaric practice seems to be growing in scope, scale, and audacity. Not only is kidnapping for ransom a crime targeted against individuals, it is an economic crime against organizations and a political weapon of terrorists. With the advent of ATMs, a new form of "express kidnapping" has emerged: The person taken hostage will be ransomed by providing his ATM card and personal identification number (PIN) to the kidnappers, who will drive around to various machines and drain as many resources as the limits of the card will allow from the victim's accounts before releasing, or killing, the victim.

Kidnapping for political concession, as took place in Afghanistan in 2007 with the kidnapping of a group of Korean Christian missionary development workers, has proven to be remarkably effective. If governments worldwide find the willpower to adopt, announce, and enforce a policy of total refusal to bargain with or make concessions to kidnappers, the scourge will begin to decline rapidly. Kidnappers rely on the inability of decent people—governments, corporations, and family members—to feel that they somehow contributed to the murder of another human, even though it is the kidnappers who create the situation, provoke the threat, and conduct the murder themselves.

The murder of reporter Daniel Pearl falls into the category of a pseudokidnapping. Daniel Pearl was murdered by a group of terrorist assassins who wanted to draw as much attention, publicity, and terror out of their cowardly act as possible. The kidnappings and videotaped beheadings that occur in Iraq, for example, are nothing more than elaborately staged murders, with the pretext of kidnapping thrown in to raise the emotional stakes.

If an organization of any kind is operating in an environment plagued by kidnapping, it needs to decide in advance what the policy toward the kidnapping will be and share that information with employees and their family members. There should be no delusions, though, that because an organization is involved in humanitarian assistance work, noncombatant neutral journalism, or is affiliated with a religious order or some world body like the U.N., that the kidnappers will behave any more humanely. Kidnappers are thieves of human beings who use their captivity to extort money. They care nothing about their victims. Some organizations elect to purchase kidnap insurance for their employees. While this can be a reasonable short-term coping strategy, in the long run such arrangements ultimately only ensure that further kidnappings will take place.

Industrial Espionage

As mentioned earlier in the chapter, intellectual property is the lifeblood of a company. The theft of that lifeblood constitutes a real and immediate threat to the mission of an organization. The first obstacle to overcome is denial—*"No one would want that information anyway . . . ."* This can only happen when the leadership works together with the security division and the workforce to engender a culture of caution and awareness. Access to production, research, marketing, sales, accounting, human resource, and other vital subfunctions of a corporation's efforts overseas should be tightly controlled. Materials to be discarded should pass the shredder test: "Give me one good reason why I shouldn't shred this." Identification cards should be worn by everyone and checked even for the most recognizable of officials. Training on the threat needs to be ongoing. Laptops, computer disks and drives, and wireless communications need to be encrypted and controlled. These actions must be taken with a sense of collective ownership over the value of protecting the intellectual property; otherwise, these actions will appear to be examples of corporate distrust for the workforce and will be resisted.

Corruption

An organization that uses bribes and succumbs to corrupt practices in the interest of expediency is opening the doors for corruption to enter into its own ranks. NGOs that have a policy of bribing local officials for access to infrastructure they need to do their business are spinning their own webs of captivity. A company that bribes politicians for business in the name of profit will soon be battling corruption within. Ethical lapses are never, ultimately, either situational or containable—these practices affect the core of the organization's structure. The implosion of Enron is a good example; even better, the collapse of one of the most prestigious and well-known accounting firms on earth—Arthur Andersen—in the wake of the scandal serves as testimony to the insidious nature of corruption.

The assertion that "this is how the game is played here" is nothing more than an anemic excuse disguised in a cross-cultural rationale. If an organization succumbs to corruption overseas, the idea that those practices will not spread within and throughout the entity are naive and, as those practices become known, the signal sent will be that short-term success is more important than the long-term mission. That's the same rationale that a group of leaders at Arthur Andersen, who knew better, used to run themselves out of business.

Embezzlement and Other Employee Crimes

Crimes of embezzlement and employee theft are particularly hard to uncover abroad because it can often be difficult to determine with any accuracy the extent of involvement of the workforce and others in a different cultural context. Close attention to regular audits and rigorous enforcement of internal controls provide reliable defensive measures. In cases where a great deal of discretionary authority must be provided to a small group of employees (or to only one individual) for the completion of the mission, such as in war zones or unstable, hostile environments, the organization must implement careful monitoring, auditing, and reconciliation from the home office. Otherwise, the cycle of unchecked power and authority is likely to lead to ever-widening abuses in situational ethics ("Normally I would never do this, but in this environment, anything goes, so . . . .")

STRATEGIES FOR INTERNATIONAL SUCCESS

There are some good, simple, effective security strategies that can help ensure mission success by balancing the risk of the organization's mission with the threats posed by the operating environment abroad. So what works? The following sections describe how good physical security, a workforce aware of security issues, surveillance detection, good relationships with the host country, and attention to current information can help an organization succeed abroad.

Good Physical Security

Investing in good physical protection in both the workplace and, where need be, in the residences of the workforce can deter and thereby avoid problems. Good quality locks on every door with redundant safety devices, closed-circuit TVs, strengthened glass windows, window and door bars or grilles, alarm systems, good lighting, a roving security patrol, and an internal public address (PA) system—with redundant radio or wireless telephone service for outlying annexes or residences—all are worthwhile investments.

Similarly, designing and building in a system of perimeter access controls is valuable not only for the actual gate control provided, but also in the signal it sends that the organization's space is controlled. Identification badges should be used to provide either electronic or security personnel-mediated access.

Access control, of course, includes computer system access and security. A disclaimer that appears when users log in that the system may be monitored provides a gentle reminder that the workplace is not an appropriate venue for online gambling or pornography. While no one likes having to remember passwords, a logon ID and frequently changed complex password provide the least expensive, most reliable protection for what is an enormous organizational investment. Some measure of protection needs to be provided for the information system itself: Investment in antiviral software, firewalls, and other protections from hackers, spammers, and other cyber thugs, particularly when the Internet service provider is less than totally reliable or is itself in development or controlled by a hostile government, is absolutely critical.

Training a Security-Competent Workforce

One of the least expensive but most effective strategies for protecting the organization's mission is to train the workforce in mitigating the threats and the organization's overall risk management strategies. The training should be presented as value adding, and should be rewarded—either through recognition or through monetary incentives structured to reinforce both *training* and *practice;* for example, the accountant who takes a refresher internal controls course *and* who demonstrates a full year of perfect internal controls practice should be financially rewarded (even if the award amount is minimal, it has enormous symbolic and behavioral value). Similarly, a warehouse manager and his staff who suffer no loss of property and have successfully completed an inventory processes training program should be rewarded. Soldiers who complete training and demonstrate competent practice should be rewarded. Even students who wholeheartedly take to the books instead of to the bars should be commended—a letter in the student's file or to her parents recognizing her mature attention to her security awareness training and her responsible behavior serves both to reinforce competent behavior and put others on warning that their lapses haven't gone without notice.

Leadership Attention, Awareness, and Priority

Any organization that delegates total responsibility for security to a corporate or organizational security officer is headed for trouble. Security awareness and attention must be an issue that the senior leadership not only endorses, but *owns.* Leaders must understand and equate safety and security with mission success. It is an ability to understand the threats and possibilities and to be alert to them, versus the need to have disaster demonstrate itself, which separates wise leaders from those who are merely managers by reaction. A university dean or provost who begins annual meetings asking about the safety and security of the student body is sending a message to the organization. A chief executive officer who demands that she and her leaders be briefed on the security of overseas operations as part of every financial review is delivering a clear message. The executive director of a humanitarian relief organization who has an insatiable need for information and updates about the security of staff on the ground is establishing a clear organizational priority. Leaders are signal senders—what they pay attention to is what gets attended to

If, on the other hand, the only person in an organization who is paying attention to security is the security officer, the leadership signal has been sent and the message is unmistakable. "We will only pay attention to security when something bad happens." This is organizational foolishness that might escape consequences in the home country, where the home field advantage lies with the organization, but it is simply courting trouble in international missions.

Surveillance Detection

In the same way that surveillance detection can provide a defensive shield of protection for individuals, organizations need to have an active program of determining, monitoring, deterring, and intercepting threats within their areas of business—the scope of internal and external forces, players, and realities that can affect mission success. For individuals, one of the tools discussed was a heightened sense of awareness—being conscious of and moving through Cooper's Colors. For the organization, it is the leadership who determines what level of caution—or color—the organization should operate within.

Some of the tools available include closed-circuit television (CCTV) monitoring, information system monitoring, audits, and internal control checks. CCTV provides the organizational equivalent to the extremely useful skill of peripheral vision, and the mere presence of a CCTV camera can deter crime and malfeasant employee behavior.

Good Relationships

Like any good guest, the organization needs to be on its best, most gracious behavior and cultivate strong, trusting relationships with the host country. Inviting key members of the host country's government and infrastructure to meetings and informal events can help bolster cooperation and lessen distrust and misunderstandings. Rather than throwing money down the rat hole of corruption and bribes, investing in representational events and sponsoring large-scale, worthwhile activities in the immediate communities are not only wise public relations strategies but effective operational expenditures.

Similarly, participating and cooperating within the local—and international—business community can pay extraordinary dividends in sharing threat information, for example. Chambers of commerce and other nation-specific enterprises can provide critical insights into key people and legal methods of getting work done. In many countries, businesses meet specifically to share security-related information and strategies. These partnerships are win-win endeavors and often cost nothing to join.

Similarly, maintaining a good, close, positive relationship with the organization's home country embassy can be invaluable. As embassy personnel tend to rotate in and out of countries, those relationships should constantly be renewed and strengthened. Having a close personal relationship with embassy officials can expedite the resolution of a wide range of normal business problems that might arise, as well as provide a stable relationship to rely on in case of a crisis or emergency.

Attention to Current Information

Finally, the leader of an effective international organization needs to be ever vigilant in scanning the horizon for new information about the threat environment, as well as for opportunities for further success. The organizational radar screen should be stretched as widely as possible to take in as much information as is potentially relevant. The more sets of organizational eyes included in that function, the greater the likelihood that an organization will be tapping not just the energy, but also the wisdom, of its employees.

CHAPTER 10

Putting Your Skills
into Practice

The previous chapters discussed the different competency areas of the Travel Wise Model. The real situations described in the first part of this chapter give you an opportunity to use the model to help analyze and clarify some noteworthy instances of international travel in the recent past.

The second part of this chapter provides an opportunity for those interested in organizational security to practice thinking through the dilemmas, confusion, and lack of information that at tend crisis management in the real world. These scenarios, unlike the situations in the first part of this chapter, are composite cases and are *not* based on actual historical events. The locations chosen for the case studies are for illustrative purposes only and do not suggest security or infrastructural weaknesses on the part of the nations or regions involved.

REAL-LIFE SITUATIONS

Michael Fay in Singapore

Eighteen-year old (U.S.) American Michael Fay, an expatriate student at Singapore International School, was arrested and charged with more than 50 counts of vandalism. He lived with his mother and stepfather in the city-state, long known for its love for order and intolerance of crime and drugs. How did a young American get into so much trouble that he had the president of the United States calling the president of Singapore to ask for leniency from his sentence of six lashes of the cane, delivered by a martial arts expert? Michael had been diagnosed with attention deficit hyperactivity disorder (ADHD)—perhaps a harbinger of trouble to come for a young man expatriating to live with a new stepfather in the highly controlled culture.

- Was this a security problem? Was it a personal and interpersonal skills issue? Would more cross-cultural training have avoided this problem?
- What was Michael's motive to be in Singapore in the first place?

NASA on Mir with the Russians

In the aftermath of the Cold War, Russia and the United States were looking for ways to build a peaceful partnership. The Russians still had the Soviet-era Mir spacecraft orbiting the earth, and it was decided that Russian cosmonauts and American astronauts would jointly operate the dilapidated craft in preparation for the joint Russian–U.S.-backed International Space Station project. Teams of three were rotated into the craft over nearly five years of partnership. During those years, space crews, typically two Russians and one U.S. American, dealt with three major crises: two blazing onboard fires, and the first motor vehicle accident in space—a supply ship rammed into the delicate space station, smashing some solar panels, breeching its integrity, and causing decompression. In many ways, the Mir was the perfect laboratory for psychological experiments in cross-cultural crisis management. Unfortunately, the lives of the three people on board were at stake. Each team member was well trained in their respective organizations, but the crews confronted the crises they faced not as one team but as two: Russian and American.

- Using the Travel Wise Model to predict the safety problems the teams would encounter, what areas of competency were at play in their crisis management attempts?
- Why couldn't the Russian and U.S. team members work together when it mattered most?

St. Mary's Study Tour in Guatemala

In January of 1998, a bus carrying 13 students and three officials from St. Mary's College in Maryland in the U.S. was held up at gunpoint by four men in a pickup truck on a lonely stretch of the Pacific Highway in Guatemala. The men robbed all of the passengers and raped five of the women. The U.S. embassy had posted a travel advisory stating that armed bandits were operating on that road, but the college had already successfully launched two similar study groups, and faculty members who accompanied the students were experienced in traveling in Guatemala and with its culture.

- Where was the competency breakdown in this tragedy?
- How could it have been avoided?
- If you were part of St. Mary's emergency response team, what would you be thinking and planning for as the students and faculty members were repatriated to the U.S.?

Natalee Holloway in Aruba/Katherine Horton in Koh Samui

These stories are tragically related. In May of 2005, U.S. American Natalee Holloway disappeared in Aruba, where she and 124 classmates were celebrating their high school graduation. Natalee, a brilliant and popular student, was last seen leaving a rowdy bar in Oranjestad with three young men. Katherine Horton was a delightful and promising Welsh third-year psychology student vacationing with friends on the island resort of Koh Samui in Thailand when her body was found floating in the water on New Year's Day, 2006. She had been raped and bludgeoned. She had just left a group of her friends to call her mom to wish her happy new year, and was walking alone down a dark and lonely stretch of the beach just after midnight when two drunken Thai fishermen assaulted her. Natalee was 18 and Katherine was 21 when their promising lives came to an end during their respective vacation travels.

- What links these two tragedies?
- What similarities in terms of the Travel Wise competencies and motivation exist, and how could these crimes have been prevented?
- If you were one of Natalee's or Katherine's travel mates, what could you have done before, during, and after the crisis to mitigate the danger and/or deal with the loss?

 **CASE STUDIES**

Keep the Travel Wise Model in mind as you read and think about the following case studies. While there are no correct solutions for these scenarios, there are rational crisis management steps that can be taken to mitigate the risk to the mission and to the personnel involved. A discussion of some of the principles involved follows the case studies at the end of this chapter. As mentioned at the beginning of this chapter, the following case studies are fictitious and are for illustrative purposes only.

Case Study 1: Kidnapping Quagmire

Petrodor Victim of Serial Extortion; Hostage Execution

Petrodor Chemicals, the Ecuador-based multinational petrochemicals giant, has become hopelessly enmeshed in a series of serial kidnapping and extortion schemes in its Amazon oil fields. Colombian-based FARC guerrillas and numerous roving bands of heavily armed bandits have taken turns at raiding Petrodor's wells, pumping facilities, and pipelines, kidnapping expatriate and local employees, and demanding extortion money even before kidnappings and attacks take place. Petrodor's Ecuadorian Puerto Este operation, a major investment in the multinational's promise to return to profitability, is in jeopardy.

Kidnapping oilfield workers and executives has long been a lucrative business in the remote Oriente region of the Amazon, between the Napo and Aguarico rivers that border Colombia, Ecuador, and Peru. But the serial method of extortion, kidnapping, and attack carried out in what appears to be an at least somewhat coordinated assault by guerilla and bandit groups represents a new phase of trouble for the company. Police and government forces seem powerless to do anything, and according to many observers, may be reluctant to get involved, if not actually profiting from the illicit activity.

To make matters worse, a locally hired employee was found murdered execution-style near a pipeline pumping station. An anonymous note was pinned to the body, saying, "Be ready to pay us or expect more bodies." Rumors have started among Petrodor's expatriate and local workforces and are spreading rapidly. The Puerto Este facility employs 43 expatriate managers, petrochemists, geologists, engineers, and riggers, and 254 locally hired workers, including a force of some 28 armed guards. Because of the poor living conditions and difficult working environment, salaries are extraordinarily high for expatriates, though somewhat less lucrative for local hires. But even the attractive salaries won't be enough to keep the workforce from leaving if something isn't done about the violence and threats of violence.

With tensions running high, an edgy workforce, and rumors abounding, a note is found by a guard patrol addressed to "Petrodor Commandante." The note demands extortion money to be paid on a monthly basis, equivalent to $25,000 U.S. dollars, or two employees will be kidnapped and held for $2 million each. It is unclear who is demanding the extortion, although details for the first payment, due in four days, are included in the note.

The vice president in charge of Puerto Este has called a meeting of the Emergency Response Group. You are to work together to develop a crisis management plan and present it to the group. Your plan should identify the mission, the issues, trip wires, options, and communications and security components.

NOTES:

Transportation

By road to Puerto Franciso: 120 kilometers over a two-lane highway. Bandits and guerillas freely attack any vehicle not in a heavily protected convoy. Air strip for Petrodor-owned Twin Otter STOL aircraft. Maximum capacity of 20 passengers.

By road to border: 18 kilometers over a two-lane road through FARC territory; cross river to Rocafuerte (in Peru). Airstrip for Petrodor-owned Twin Otter STOL aircraft. Landing and flyover rights must be negotiated with Peruvian government. Maximum capacity of 20 passengers.

Guard force

28 lightly armed (MK-4 automatic assault rifles; SIG-Sauer 9mm automatic sidearms), locally trained and hired security guards, commanded by a former Ecuadorian military colonel who has good connections to local police and military units.

Communications

Cell phones (operate only when booster/relay station intact; is vulnerable to attack and has frequently been disabled); 116 short-wave radio sets; two satellite phones.

Emergency Response Group

Puerto Este VP, Director of Operations

Director of Security

Oilfield Chief

Director, Administrative and Financial Operations

1. What is the mission of Petrodor's Puerto Este facility?
2. What is the value of that mission?
3. What are the most pressing security issues?
4. What are some rational trip wires for action?
5. What options exist?
6. What can be done to manage communication?
7. What can be done to lower the risk?

Case Study 2: Industrial Catastrophe

ViroTech Level IV Containment Breeched in Shenyang Lab

ViroTech, a NASDAQ-listed eight-year-old company had experienced explosive growth in every quarter until the last two years. Early patents that capitalized the company with huge sums for research reinvestment have been dwindling, and the new pharmaceutical mass production facility in Shenyang has been eating up enormous amounts of capital and crippling the company's cash flow. All bets are on the profitability of the Shenyang facility's mass production of human interferon, insulin, and a promising new human stem cell-produced retroviral inhibitor, Antinal. Production of insulin has started but quality problems plagued the first batches. The interferon is due to be shipped in three weeks, and everyone has been working double shifts to make the delivery deadlines that would keep ViroTech afloat. The very expensive Level IV containment facility, necessary for the highly controversial and technically exacting production method for Antinal, has been under pressure to produce some indication of a realistic first production deadline. The tech sector market analysts have been watching closely, and the value of ViroTech stock (and its ability to raise capital to pay off loans) has been riding on a market eager for good news on Antinal.

This morning, the alarm sounded in the building housing the Level IV containment lab. A micropore membrane filter had torn and exposed workers in the facility to the highly virulent Variola Mosaic Virus (VMV). The unattenuated virus is used as a carrier for the introduction of engineered gene plasmids into human embryonic stem cells. The stem cells normally start producing Antinal, a highly effective retroviral agent that then neutralizes the VMV carrier. The Antinal can then be extracted and used as a highly effective agent against HIV and other immunotoxic viral diseases.

The seven workers in the Level IV containment lab at the time had a near 100 percent chance of exposure to the potentially fatal VMV. There were no workers in the Level III area surrounding the lab. Twelve people in the Level II minimum exposure area risked no more than a 20 percent chance of exposure, and an additional 58 technicians in the Level I area were exposed to a less than 1 percent chance of contact with the virus.

Following standard protocol, the building was sealed, the ventilators shut down, and the workers confined in their respective containment areas. The project's liaison officer for the Government of China (GOC) was at the facility when the accident occurred and contacted the Chinese authority. The Chinese deployed 1,400 fully armed Red Army troops wearing paper masks to ring the facility in a security cordon. They are allowing no one in or out of the compound. Workers on the facility who were not in the containment building have been ordered to return to their quarters until further notice.

An AP reporter who was traveling through Shenyang has already filed a story that is hitting the AP wire describing the incident as a "massive infectious Frankenstein." The reporter has been calling into the plant's Public and Community Relations office for an interview. Local TV stations have picked up the story and are doing on-the-spot interviews with an inexhaustible supply of angry Chinese citizens in the neighborhood, demanding the government shut down the American "monster" factory.

The Vice President for Operations has convened ViroTech's Crisis Action Team. You are to discuss the threat to your mission, the issues, set trip wires, develop a crisis management plan including communicating with employees and the home office, public relations, the GOC, emergency logistics, and everything else needed to manage the crisis. You will be presenting your plan via a videoconference to your home office.

1. What is the mission of the ViroTech plant in Shenyang?
2. What is the value of the mission?
3. What are some rational trip wires to guide decision making?
4. What options are available to the crisis management group?
5. Describe the communication programs you would put in place to handle communication within the plant, within the community and the GOC, and to the ViroTech home office.

Case Study 3: SARs Revisits Asia

Taipei Office of O'Connor & Baldrich Faces Crisis

Panic is starting to spread throughout the expatriot community in Taipei, the capital of Taiwan. The bustling Asian market has been paralyzed with fears of another outbreak of the Sudden Acute Respiratory Syndrome (SARS) virus, and the government has taken the unprecedented step of sealing the borders and not permitting Taiwanese nationals to either leave or enter the country. Expatriates with valid visas are being allowed to exit, as long as they can pass the "routine" health inspection at the airport, but no foreigners are being allowed into the country.

The Taipei office of O'Connor & Baldrich, a Big Five multinational accounting firm with a local expatriate workforce of 213 employees and 278 family members, is under pressure from its professional staff to evacuate. Corporate headquarters in London has made it known that, to the extent possible, the company prefers that its critical Taipei office stand pat, as it seems on the verge of a breakthrough in the market. It has left the final decision on evacuation, however, to the Taipei Office Director. The Government of Taiwan (GOT) has made it very clear that as far as it is concerned, there is no epidemic and any action that would be seen as running contrary to that assessment would be viewed unfavorably. Relations with the GOT are critical to success—although an open and free market thrives, cooperation from the government is critical to marketplace viability.

So far there have been three reported deaths and 12 more confirmed cases, scattered in a seemingly random pattern around the congested city. An unusually high number of children at the British International School (BIS) have reported in sick, but it is unclear if they are actually sick or just being kept home by worried parents. Almost all the school-aged dependents of O&B's largely British, Irish, and American workforce attend BIS. The school also employs four company spouses. Rumors are starting to spread quickly about the severity of the outbreak.

A tough decision must be made. If O'Connor and Baldrich evacuates its employees prematurely, it is sure to compromise its mission by antagonizing its relationship with the GOT. If it waits too long and a real epidemic develops, the borders will be totally sealed—no air carrier would agree to take people out, nor would there be any port willing to have them in transit or as final destination passengers. If one or more of O&B's staff were to succumb to the virus, it would be an immeasurable personal and financial disaster for the whole office.

An Emergency Response Team meeting of O'Connor and Baldrich's top managers is convened. You are to discuss the threat to your mission, the issues, set trip wires, develop a crisis management plan including decision tripwires for conditions under which a full evacuation would be ordered, communicating with employees, family members and the home office, public relations, the Government of Taiwan, emergency logistics, and everything else needed to manage the crisis. You will be presenting your plan via a videoconference to the London office.

1. What are the issues affecting O&B's mission in Taiwan? What is O&B's mission?
2. Who are the stakeholders involved in the crisis?
3. What are some rational trip wires to guide the evacuation debate?
4. What options are available to the crisis management group?

Case Study 4: Humanitarian Fiasco

Humanitarian Aid Worker Attacked

The International Committee of the Red Cross (ICRC) has committed to a massive emergency relief effort on the contested Ethiopian/Eritrean border, the site of tremendous suffering due to the East African drought. Conflict between the two nations continues at a low but vicious level as each side has accused the other of poisoning extremely scare supplies of water in the dispute. Renegade soldiers on each side have been accused of raping and murdering impoverished villagers who are hanging onto life by the thinnest of threads.

The crisis is centered in the Denakil desert, a below-sea-level depression whose disputed boundaries are part of the cause of the conflict. Scarcity of water and food, tribal territorialism, and a lack of any of civil society's institutions complicate recovery efforts. The impoverished live essentially without a meaningful political administration, justice system, school system, police force, or even the most basic citizen services. The United Nations has predicted that one million people are in imminent danger of dying unless emergency aid is delivered immediately.

Although both the Eritrean and Ethiopian governments claim they welcome foreign disaster assistance for the area, in fact, both governments have redirected critical donated aid supplies to their armies. The Eritreans have denied seaport access for food aid bound for landlocked Ethiopia, and the Ethiopians have staged military raids on Eritrean food distribution centers.

To staunch the humanitarian crisis, the ICRC has contracted a Russian cargo carrier to fly huge Tupolevs into the Denakil and offload cargo directly into three makeshift ICRC-run distribution centers in the desert. The centers are staffed by "disaster circuit riders" who have volunteered to work in what is a nonpermissive and very dangerous environment. The policy of the ICRC is to withdraw its workers when continued service would unduly jeopardize their safety, or when combatants have declared hostility or acted with hostile intent toward the ICRC or its members.

The ICRC's Denakil food distribution centers are clearly saving masses of people from starvation. Intensive rehydration has saved countless children on the brink of death. But, on Thursday of last week, at the Denakil East distribution site, an Eritrean troop convoy came into the center and transloaded the contents of a Tupolev onto their trucks at gunpoint. They shot to death three nomads who were awaiting rations, and wounded an Italian ICRC worker. Today, at the Adigrat (north) site, Ethiopian troops ransacked supplies that had been offloaded and set fire to three tons of grain that had been stacked in burlap sacks. When women who had come to the site to claim extra food for their starving children began yelling and throwing stones at the troops, the troops opened fire on the women, killing 13 and dragging off another eight with them, over the vehement protests of the ICRC workers. One worker who attempted to pull a hostage out of a military truck was hit with a rifle butt and lost an eye.

The ICRC Denakil Project Director has called a meeting of the leaders of the three distribution centers to discuss the crisis. You are to discuss the threat to your mission, the issues involved, determine trip wires, develop a crisis management plan including communicating with the workers and ICRC headquarters, the respective governments, and the international news media. Discuss options and come to agreement on a recommended course of action.

1. Does the incident at the Adigrat site indicate a mandatory withdrawal/evacuation of staff?
2. What are the global mission implications for ICRC if workers are withdrawn?
3. Describe an effective communications plan to both share information and influence outcomes.

CASE STUDY REVIEWS

The following reviews are intended as a cross check for your own thinking and analysis in the organizational case studies. There are no definitive right answers—only principles and some salient points that would arise as predictable issues. In all cases, though, keep in mind that emotions will be part of the problems—and of the solutions.

Case Study 1: Kidnapping Quagmire

The mission of Petrodor's Puerto Este facility is to produce oil revenues to return Petrodor to profitability. Petrodor's Ecuadorian Puerto Este operation, a major investment in the multinational's mission, is in jeopardy. The operation, which is clearly critical to Petrodor's survival, represents both a big investment and the hope for the company's future. Against the weight of this organizational value, pulling the plug on the operation would be a disaster. More risk will have to be endured.

The most pressing security issues include an active, substantiated, serial kidnap/extortion/murder threat with an impending deadline. Additionally, rumor control and communication with the workforce and stakeholders must be managed. Keeping the workforce, both expatriate and local, fully informed engenders trust and cooperation. An "all hands" meeting should be arranged and repeated at least several times per week.

Since it is still uncertain who the perpetrators include, but it is clear that they are prepared to carry out their threats, the extortion threat should be taken at face value—they will kidnap and kill if extortion money is not paid. The reality of this scenario is that it takes place because the government is unable, or unwilling, to commit the resources to control the region. There is no way out of this situation without direct government support. An important trip wire for decision making becomes the government's actions to support Petrodor.

Of the options that exist, the two that should be excluded first are doing nothing, which will invite kidnapping, murder, and the exodus of the workforce, and fully acceding to the extortionists' demands, which will simply invite continued and perhaps further intolerable demands on the facility. Two other options are intertwined: the first is to seek immediate government action using all of the political, economic, and personal ties available to compel military intervention. The government must be shown that the alternatives—ensuring private funding for a terrorist group in its midst, or abandoning the facility and the region, are untenable and disastrous for the nation. Every effort must be made to convey a sense of do-or-die urgency. If the government is slow or continues to remain unwilling to act, Petrodor must reinforce its own security operations with additional security personnel and more aggressive self-defensive measures.

The communications part of the puzzle requires full-time, ongoing attention. Petrodor must open direct lines of communication with the government to ensure that the issue remains in the forefront of the political process. Here, the press can be an ally into pushing or shaming the government into action. Contact with the press should frame the issue as one of the government's abandonment of its responsibilities, and not as a refusal to protect the profit interest of a private sector concern. Communication within the Petrodor community should be managed through all-hands meetings, daily security updates and reminders, and open opportunities for the members of the workforce to share opinions and ideas, as well as voice their own fear and frustrations. Communications with Petrodor's headquarters should be nearly constant: It may be useful to keep an open line between the facility and the home office to both relay information and to maintain a sense of urgency, but also of control. Communication with the extortionists, if it takes place at all, should be carefully managed and enacted only with an agreed upon specific strategy.

Other actions to immediately lower the risk include hiring more guards, setting out more patrols in larger numbers, activating an alert system, conducting frequent radio checks, preparing contingency plans, escape routes, supplies, permissions, and charters, and considering an incentive package for those workers who commit to staying the course.

Case Study 2: Industrial Catastrophe

The ViroTech plant in Shenyang is vital to the company's future and survival in a fast moving industry, where opportunities and competition quickly reward winners and punish the slow to respond or produce. The value of ViroTech's effort in its Shenyang plant could mean the difference between survival or ruin. In high-tech, high-risk production facilities, accidents will happen. They must be corrected with dispatch and new procedures put into place to reassure workers and the community that this problem won't occur again. The key to understanding this problem is to recognize that it is fundamentally a problem of fear and communication.

Continued isolation and the successful treatment of all of those impacted in the lab itself is just one part of the problem. The larger and more persistent issue will be with the fear that the episode has generated within the workforce, the larger Chinese community in and around the plant, and with stockholders and market analysts around the world. Fear can never be managed by being tight lipped. Every effort must be made to (1) reassure the public that there is no danger to anyone outside the lab (conducting a press conference immediately outside the lab in question will help); (2) carefully describe what happened, why it happened, and what is being done to resolve the situation and make sure it never happens again; (3) publicly own responsibility and state that ViroTech will pay for any damages that anyone incurs as the result of the event; (4) demonstrate ViroTech's sincere and profound concern over the prognosis of its infected workers and demonstrate that no expense will be spared to help them recover; (5) use the news conference forum to reassure the news media that they will be kept abreast of every and any development in the situation; and (6) use the news conference to describe to stockholders, analysts, and the public the progress being made on the work being done in the lab, and its importance to consumers worldwide—that this work is on the front lines of dealing with the global epidemic of HIV and other viral pandemic diseases.

ViroTech should set up daily press conferences and invite interested members of the national and international press: Bombard them with nice-looking reprintable graphics of the progress and machinery of lifesaving pharmaceuticals, background stories on some of the researchers, their degrees and qualifications, and sidebar stories of successful products that the company has already produced. Openness to the press should be so complete that the ViroTech's home office should be able to get most of the information they need from watching the daily public press conferences.

Case Study 3: SARs Revisits Asia

O'Connor & Baldrich's main quandary is one of dealing with fear, trust, and preserving vital, but delicate, relationships. As a first step, a community meeting—perhaps in the format of a town hall meeting—should be organized. The situation and O&B's take on it should be fully described and explained. O&B employees and family members should be offered an opportunity to evacuate if they so choose, with the leadership clearly stating that they intend to stay and ride out the threat, trusting in the Government of Taiwan's ability to deal with the medical and epidemiological threat. This public meeting could be broadcast as a videoconference to the London home office of O&B.

Since O'Connor & Baldrich's success is tied to its relationship with the GOT, and the GOT has indicated its position, O&B should find an appropriate public forum—perhaps a press release—to declare its agreement with the GOT's analysis and faith in its ability to handle the issue. There is no need to mention who or how many employees and family members might take the opportunity to evacuate. The reality is the work force and family members are probably safer following some simple precautions to stay where they are than they would be if they decided to return to their homes in the United States or the British Isles—a 30-hour return trip on a flight that simply recirculates the same air to all of the passengers is a risk in itself.

Case Study 4: Humanitarian Fiasco

As with all humanitarian assistance problems, the balance between human empathy and political reality is tested in profoundly difficult ways. A key question to resolve is to interpret the incident that occurred and blinded the ICRC employee against the organization's stated policy—its public trip wire. Was the employee targeted, or was he the victim of nonspecific violence? One of the initial steps to take is to gather as much information as possible to determine what exactly happened and why. These deliberations need to include decision makers at ICRC headquarters, and they also need to be shared with the ICRC workers in the field. The disaster circuit riders should be offered an opportunity to decide for themselves whether they want to continue in their work or not, without penalty. Regardless of their personal decisions, their input into the larger decision for ICRC is also important: Should the organization stay and try to continue their work or pull up stakes and abandon the project? Because the incident could happen again with the personnel of either government, the ICRC might consider holding a press conference and invite members of the international press corps, not to embarrass either government, but to put them both on notice that the world is watching what is going on, and that there will be consequences—at least in the eyes of public opinion about the two regimes and, importantly, which one the world may begin to see as the bad guys.

SPECIAL ISSUES

Managing Students & Young Adults/Professionals

At this point, if you've read this book and gone through your own Travel Wise Personal Inventory, you've hopefully come across not only some new ideas and a model to help guide your thinking about international safety and security, but perhaps your attitude has also shifted. These ideas, and that shift in attitude, will serve you well as you embark upon or continue with your personal journeys around the world. The Travel Wise Model provides a solid and holistic starting point for analyzing the risk and safeguarding your travels, but there are some special topics that deserve brief mention. A discussion of managing the travels of students and young professionals, traveling with pets, and the dynamics of coming home conclude this book.

There are two remarkable features in dealing with the safety and security of expatriating young adults: (1) younger travelers tend to still be in the formative stages of their own identities and of understanding who they are, and (2) they tend to have less of an experiential base to draw upon. Pretending these issues are already resolved or somewhat beyond the control of the program sponsors or administrators is doing an injustice to all involved.

Part of predeparture and in-country orientation programs should include asking the sojourners *who they want to be* as members of a global community. Cross-cultural and interpersonal skills training sessions should include reflective activities, like journaling, not only to document learnings, but also to push the traveler to begin to develop an international identity construct; a *personae* that is defined by a sense of ethics, maturity, responsibility, and morality. What does that have to do with safety and security? Everything. Students who are guided by their own constructs instead of *reacting against* someone else's are more likely to make good choices about their behavior.

The second part of the reality is a bit trickier. Lack of experience can be quite a disadvantage, for example, when a young person is negotiating romantic relationships across cultures; when determining whether it might not be all that bad to have one last beer at a bar when there isn't much familiarity with drinking in any context; when deciding what is safe and what isn't. I encourage trainers and administrators to actively incorporate new learnings by using experiential methods: "You shared with us that you went to the bar and decided to have one last beer. So what happened after that and what did it mean? What will you do next time?" These types of check-in experiences can help young people develop their own behavioral constructs without external judgments or directions.

TRAVELING WITH PETS

In working with international travelers, one area that never ceases to amaze me is the relationship some owners have with their pets. People who travel with pets are asking for some additional logistics challenges, and they need to be aware of the expense and occasional inconvenience of traveling with pets. This is an area in which acting on assumptions on how things ought to work—instead of carefully researching how they do work—can lead to considerable heartache. That said, if a pet is important to a traveler's happiness and personal success, and the traveler is willing to be a responsible, informed co-traveler, there is no reason not to take Fido or Fifi.

The first things to check are airline flight regulations and policies—these can change overnight!—as well as the animal control policies in the destination country. Some countries insist on a quarantine period, and the pet will be held in isolation to ensure it is not carrying disease into the country. This is, of course, at the expense of the owner, and it is never negotiable. Proof of required veterinary immunizations may also have to be hand-carried.

Carrying pets to areas that are less stable becomes more of a challenge. In the event of the need for a rapid evacuation—the August 2006 evacuation of most expatriates from Lebanon during the Israeli invasion is a good example—pets can greatly complicate urgent travel arrangements. Just when normalcy and stability seemed to be returning to that troubled country, and a number of Lebanese who emigrated to the British Isles, Canada, and the U.S. during the era of the civil war began returning—with pets—the need arose for a hasty departure. Many were faced with a very unhappy choice—abandon their pets or stay in country.

A further complication to keep in mind, particularly if the pet will be unaccompanied and/or placed in the cargo hold of an aircraft, is the possibility of an unanticipated flight delay. An animal in a cage in the belly of an aircraft can have a very rough time of it if the plane is forced to spend long hours on a hot tarmac.

COMING HOME

In dealing with travelers for almost 30 years, one generalization that has particular validity is that most travelers prepare much more for going abroad than they do for returning home, and this causes their repatriation to be more difficult than it need be. Why bother to prepare for returning home? The assumption is that the individual's home is something static that has stayed safely locked in a time vault of close friends, predictable services, and reliable access to meeting one's needs, and it awaits to be recaptured from one's memory and translated into ongoing reality.

The individual who has been abroad for a considerable length of time has experienced the changes he has gone through on an incremental basis, and barely has had time—or perspective—to notice that he has changed at all. The fact is, though, that travel does change people. Individuals are rarely able to understand the scope and dimensions of the changes in themselves until they have a chance to compare who they've become with the environment from which they came. This process can take some time—and can cause some uncomfortable readjustments.

Life back home can seem less exciting and interesting than life overseas. For business travelers, often the status and prestige they enjoyed overseas is diminished as they come back into the corporate maw of hundreds of others who have similar rank and stature. They suddenly feel less important, and that identity challenge can be disorienting. The favorite restaurant that was the subject of such longings overseas just doesn't seem to measure up to one's exalted memory of it. Friendships and relationships that had been close and sustaining now feel awkward and distant. Questions like, *"So, how were your three years in China?"* seem to neither be answerable nor want a real answer.

Why does this matter to the traveler? Part of the idea of mission success was to go abroad, do something with a goal in mind, and return having accomplished that goal. Returning to a land that doesn't seem to be interested in the travel or care about the accomplishment of the goal can be disconcerting and diminish the experience for the traveler. Knowing that these phenomena are predictable is the best immunization against re-entry shock.

APPENDIX

Information Strategies and Resources

There are amazing resources available to travelers to inform their preparations and help shape realistic expectations of what they are likely to face abroad. Here are some very easy to use, free resources on the world wide web.

The U.S. Department of State's web site for travelers has a number of resources that are invaluable for travelers, including advice for specific groups and issues and travel advisories. www.travel.state.gov

The Overseas Security Advisory Council (www.osac.gov) is the product of a unique collaboration between the U.S. private sector, academic institutions, and the Department of State's Bureau of Diplomatic Security.

The British Government's Travel Advice, available through www.fco.gov.uk, is a goldmine of security and cultural information.

The Canadian Department of Foreign Affairs and Trade hosts www.dfait-maeci.gc.ca, including the invaluable Travel Reports and Warnings.

Perhaps the most valuable and comprehensive site for students and academic program administrators is the Center for Global Education's SAFETI Clearinghouse site at www.globaled .us/safeti—it has everything—including training and countless other links to use as an initial point of entry to research.

A number of private security companies have excellent websites and provide information unvarnished by political and diplomatic considerations.

Kroll (www.kroll.com)
Pinkerton (www.ci-pinkerton.com)

There are also a number of online resources for learning about your emotional intelligence—some are free, but readers are cautioned to verify the reliability and trustworthiness of those sites before you provide any information about yourself. A number of reliable statistically normed self scoring instruments are also available at modest cost.

In short, there is no shortage of information anymore. And there is no excuse for not doing your homework. That's what Travel Wise is all about.

ABOUT THE AUTHOR

Ray S. Leki has been a leader in work force expatriation and security training for more than 20 years. He is an adjunct professor at American University's School of International Service and teaches graduate classes in personal and organizational security, negotiation, intercultural facilitation and training, and spirituality and conflict transformation. For the past 15 years, he has led the U.S. Department of State's Transition Center and Overseas Briefing Center, and overseen and developed the Foreign Service Institute's Security Overseas Seminars program, training scores of thousands of diplomats, government employees, and family members in overseas security awareness. He has produced videos on overseas security, well-being, and crisis response for the U.S. foreign affairs community and has designed computer-based and countless conventional training programs.

Prior to working at American University and the Foreign Service Institute, Ray was a Peace Corps volunteer and staff member for 10 years, overseeing stateside and international training and serving abroad in Nepal (twice), in Pakistan, and in Poland. Ray has a Masters degree in Leadership from Georgetown University's McDonough School of Business, and is a graduate of the Foreign Affairs Leadership Seminar, Harvard's John F. Kennedy School's executive development programs, National Security Council's Security Educator's program, and a variety of security training and other courses at the Department of State and the Central Intelligence Agency.

Ray is an advisory board member of SIETAR-DC, the Foreign Affairs Youth Foundation, the Intercultural Management Institute, and the Association for International Protocol Consultants.

He is a frequent speaker at international conferences including the American Society for Training and Development (ASTD); the Employee Relocation Council; the Society for Intercultural Education, Training, and Research (SIETAR); Society for Applied Learning Technology; the National Foreign Trade Council; the International Banking Association; and others. He is the recipient of four superior honor and numerous other government awards, and is a co-recipient of the Beyond War Award. Ray lives in Fairfax, Virginia, with his wife and daughters.

INDEX

British Government's Travel Advice,
207
Bushnell, Prudence, 176

C

Canadian Department of Ministry of
Foreign Affairs and Trade, 207
case studies, 185–202
cell phones, 55, 61, 77
Center for Global Education SAFETI
Clearinghouse, 207
charpis, 110–111
chemical weapons, 144–146
child rearing, 62–63, 74–75, 105
cultural socialization in, 107–108
children, third-culture, 102
civil disorder, 140
closed-circuit television (CCTV),
183
communication
cell phones in, 55, 61, 77
in crisis management, 123–125
emergency plan for, 34, 76–77
organizational, 174–176
with other travelers, 159–160
in Petrodor case study, 198–199
companionship, 31–32, 60–63. *See
also* relationships; sex
security skills for women and,
149–155
competence, cultural, 113–114
composure, 96–97
conflict, comfort with, 32, 68–69
conformity, 101
Cooper's Colors/Cooper Color Code,
118–119, 123, 183
corruption, 121–122, 139, 179–180
Country Reports on Terrorism, 177
cover-ups, 174–175
credit cards, 71

crime, 138
employee, 180
experience with, 129–130
foreigners as targets of, 100–101
Crisis Leadership (Klann), 176
crisis management, 123–125
communication in, 174–176
organizational, 173–174
cross-cultural skills, 16–17, 99–114
benefits of, 113–114
culture-generic, 19–20
international/developing world
experience, 34–35, 101–102
language skills, 35, 102–104
learning about cultures, 106–113
marriage and, 105–106
motivation and, 166
self-assessment of, 34–35
in Travel Wise Model, 18–19
urban living, 34, 100–101
cultural competence, 113–114
culture contrast model, 89
cultures
adaptability and, 112–113
definition of, 106–107
interest in target, 110–112
learning about other, 106–113
socialization in, 107–108
customer perspectives, 171
Cuzco, Peru, 132

D

dangerous cities, list of, 101
death
preparation for, 78–81
will preparation, 33, 34, 72–73, 76
de Becker, Gavin, 117
decision-making process, 12–15. *See
also* risk assessment
DeMello, Cjetan, 89